LINCOLN,

KEEP WEEDING BY EXAMPLE!

Growing Weeders into Leaders

Leadership Lessons from the Ground Level

1/30/18

BOOK ENDORSEMENTS FOR

Growing Weeders into Leaders

In his "how to" guide, Jeff McManus, gives a perspective on service and leadership from the ground up. As a member of the leadership team at Chick-fil-A, part of my job is to help define the future of our business. We have addressed the fact that success is all about succession, and that in order to ensure future success you need to be constantly growing the leaders around you. One thing we have learned throughout my tenure at Chick-fil-A is that there's a big difference between locating leaders and cultivating them. Jeff reminds us that all leaders can be cultivated with the right pruning and nurturing…this book will serve as a guide for doing just that. Perfect for all current and future leaders.

Dan T. Cathy, CEO Chick-fil-A, Inc.

Refreshing, innovative and creative are the words that came to mind as I read this book. *Growing Weeders into Leaders* gently shows the positive end result of trusting, respecting and complimenting people who are doing 'manual' labor. As a valued department at Ole Miss, Jeff's team has proven their ability to 'make a place look loved' and to attract world-class athletes, faculty and other top-notch talent to that campus as a result.

Dan Miller, New York Times bestselling author
48 Days to the Work You Love

After helping transform the Ole Miss campus from a former beauty into what is frequently hailed as the country's most stunning, Jeff McManus knows a few things about building an award-winning team. Far more than a dry collection of management tips, *Growing Weeders into Leaders* is filled with personal experiences and insights aimed at empowering employees and helping them unleash their own creativity and drive. No matter what business you're in, Jeff can help your team reach its full potential.

Jeffrey S. Vitter, Chancellor and Distinguished Professor
University of Mississippi

I love the intentional approach of this book. Perhaps unintended, but Jeff has it figured out—our society has made 'leadership' too big and way too complicated. Thus he puts us through a simple approach that people come first. His leadership has helped to propel our university from good to great—in not only physical beauty but in attitude and culture. I love working with Jeff and his team. I am glad he has chosen to make his approach available and accessible in such an enjoyable read.

Ross Bjork, Vice Chancellor for Intercollegiate Athletics
The University of Mississippi

For me, being in the landscape industry, *Growing Weeders into Leaders* is a true treat. I could not put it down and actually read it twice! What you will find in this book is a gifted writer with an ability to simplify what so many folks try and make difficult. You will be truly inspired by the natural way Jeff shares leadership lessons for growing successful leaders in any industry. Great book!

Cary Avery, CGM University of California, Davis

For generations stories have been used to give meaning to who we are and what we believe in. Throughout "Growing Weeders into Leaders" Jeff McManus brilliantly uses the art of storytelling to describe the many complex concepts of positive leadership. This book is rich with examples of how an effective leader empowers others and encourages them to lead. Great work!

Katie Wilson, Deputy Under Secretary for Food, Nutrition, and Consumer Services, USDA - Former Executive Director of the National Food Service Management Institute

Growing Weeders into Leaders isn't, as it first appears, a book about leadership development in the landscape industry. The practices shared in the book are relevant to any type of organization. With our facilities in the same town, my team and I have benefitted greatly from Jeff's teachings and we are stronger because of it.

Mark McAnally, Quality Manager, Caterpillar HPE, Oxford, MS

Growing Weeders into Leaders reminds us that great leadership is a quest for excellence, not only in ourselves, but in our teams and in our work. Jeff McManus has coached my colleagues in the classroom on how to create winning teams, and now he has brought that same leadership wisdom to the page in this easy to digest book, full of true-life leadership stories. No matter the industry, the lessons transfer seamlessly, a gentle reminder that at the end of the day, leadership is all about investing in people.

Bethany Cooper, Human Resources Business Partner FNC, Inc.

Jeff is an inspirational leader, speaker and writer. *Growing Weeders into Leaders* is a straightforward approach to problem solving and methods to grow individuals into a team. Jeff is an excellent teacher of new leaders and is quick to encourage experienced leaders to trust our instincts. Sometimes we just need reminding of the principles that have positive results and keep moving forward.

Susanne Woodell, CGM Historic Gardens Manager, BILTMORE

I found *Growing Weeders Into Leaders* an inspiring and accurate reflection of the challenges involved with managing the landscape and facilities of a comprehensive higher education institution. I enjoyed and appreciated Jeff's candor and innovation in cultivating leadership within his organization. His work clearly demonstrates the impact of genuine, caring leadership on the development and success of an organization. This is a must-read for anyone or any industry looking to impact the lives of others in a positive way!

Dr. Chris Crenshaw, Associate Vice President for Facilities Planning Management, The University of Southern Mississippi

Jeff is a man of integrity and a leader in the landscape industry. Having met several of Jeff's team members through the years it is obvious this book is based on real life activity in the landscape department at the University of Mississippi. I have been in the landscape industry for over 40 years and I learned things from reading this book that I can easily use—as well as some things that will require a bit more planning and discipline. Everyone in a leadership role would benefit from following the principles presented in this book.

John A. Burns, CGM, Landscape Manager, Past President, Professional Grounds Management Society, University of Texas at Austin

I have been coming to Oxford for the better part of 40 years, and can speak firsthand to the tremendous improvement that the University of Mississippi's campus has seen under the leadership of Jeff McManus. It is no accident that the campus has been recognized as most beautiful on five separate occasions, and when you read this book, you'll see why. Jeff's leadership principles and philosophies discussed in this book can take any size business or workforce and turn them into a truly unified team that is highly motivated to achieve success. I have had the privilege of hearing Jeff speak on two separate occasions and I highly recommend him – the only thing better than the book is Jeff in person!

Ward Toler, Market Manager, C Spire

My good friend, Jeff McManus, has planted in words in the same incredible way he has planted in the grounds of Ole Miss, making the invisible become visible, allowing others to see the rich talent he has been given. From the landscape architect of the most beautiful campus in America comes now the author inspiring us to become all we can be in the fields God has placed us.

Lee Paris, CEO Meadowbrook Capital, LLC.

Jeff's book may be about landscape management, but the techniques he employs and teaches are transferrable to any industry or team. McManus teaches a system with identifiable objectives, measurement techniques, and easily communicated team principles. This is a book for leaders at any stage of their development.

Campbell McCool, Former CEO, McCool Communications - Founder and Developer of Plein Air

As a fan of books geared toward insight and professional advancement, I greatly enjoyed Jeff McManus' *Growing Weeders into Leaders.* His stories and self-reflection guide us in understanding how we are growing our own teams. You might think the world of commercial real estate brokerage would operate differently from a landscape team, but Jeff has shown me that in *all* cases, in all businesses, we are very much the same. Jeff's work with my team has utilized the guiding principles addressed in his book and both are clear, insightful guidance toward professional development in any industry.

Elizabeth J. Randall, President
Randall Commercial Group

GROWING
WEEDERS
INTO
LEADERS

Leadership Lessons
from the Ground Level

JEFF MCMANUS

NEW YORK

NASHVILLE • MELBOURNE • VANCOUVER

Growing Weeders into Leaders

Leadership Lessons *from the* Ground Level

Published in New York, New York, by Morgan James Publishing. Morgan James and The Entrepreneurial Publisher are trademarks of Morgan James, LLC.
www.MorganJamesPublishing.com

The Morgan James Speakers Group can bring authors to your live event. For more information or to book an event visit The Morgan James Speakers Group at www.TheMorganJamesSpeakersGroup.com.

Shelfie

A **free** eBook edition is available with the purchase of this print book.

CLEARLY PRINT YOUR NAME ABOVE IN UPPER CASE

Instructions to claim your free eBook edition:
1. Download the Shelfie app for Android or iOS
2. Write your name in **UPPER CASE** above
3. Use the Shelfie app to submit a photo
4. Download your eBook to any device

ISBN 9781683503309 paperback
ISBN 9781683503323 eBook
Library of Congress Control Number:
2016918397

Cover Design by:
Chris Treccani
www.3dogdesign.net

Interior Design by:
Chris Treccani
www.3dogdesign.net

Morgan James
The Entrepreneurial Publisher™

Builds

with...

Habitat for Humanity®
Peninsula and
Greater Williamsburg

In an effort to support local communities, raise awareness and funds, Morgan James Publishing donates a percentage of all book sales for the life of each book to Habitat for Humanity Peninsula and Greater Williamsburg.

Get involved today! Visit
www.MorganJamesBuilds.com

DEDICATION

This book is dedicated in loving memory to my mother, Jane McManus. Her gentle confidence, self-sacrifice and her daily expression of Christian faith and love was (and is) an inspiration and comfort. I love you.

TABLE OF CONTENTS

FOREWORD

Jeff McManus arrived on our campus as 36-year-old well educated, attractive man with a lovely wife and three young boys with a fourth soon to follow. He quickly won my confidence as well as that of his colleagues and leaders across the University. In our initial interview he told me he would give us a 5-star campus if we would provide him with a pick-up truck and if he could report to me. We shook hands, he and his family came and the transformation of our campus landscape was underway.

He organized his staff, laid out his **plans** and **challenged** them to develop the **best-landscaped campus in America**. They **succeeded**…Jeff, his family and his staff. **Attrition reduced his staff by seven**; He asked if he could use those funds to **increase the compensation of those who remained**. He asked if he could put them in **attractive uniforms**. He asked if he could purchase **additional items for more ease and expedition of labor**.

He challenged his staff to "own" the campus. He created teams such as **"delta force," "all stars," "the rough riders"** and provided motivational information and guidance. He coined the phrase **"weeders to leaders."** The staff bought in and became highly respected…and gained self-respect.

In this book he clearly leads the reader down the path to success that he and his staff have followed. The town of Oxford joined him in his effort to reach and sustain excellence and is a much more attractive community. Jeff is an award winning leader, a successful writer and motivational speaker. I commend this book, and him, to you.

Robert C. Khayat
Chancellor Emeritus
The University of Mississippi

ACKNOWLEDGMENTS

This book would not be possible without the assistance of so many family, friends and supporters. The following listing of thanks skims the surface:

- Thank you to my wife, Suzanne McManus, who supported all my efforts, read chapters, gave feedback and remained my wife. I love you.
- Thank you to all four of my sons for their support, their commentary and their humor (especially the humor!).
- Thank you to my Dad, Garey McManus. You taught me so much and never ceased to invest in my potential.
- To my brother Craig and sister Janet Russell, I am thankful for your continuous support and encouragement.
- Thank you to Benita Whitehorn for her patient editorial process.

- To JoAnn Edwards for coaching, editing, suggesting and supporting.
- To Larry Sparks, Mark Hartnett, Lee Paris, Ron Wilson, and Sam McManus for being honest and open sounding boards throughout this journey.
- To former Chancellor Dan Jones and current Chancellor Jeffrey Vitter for embracing the landscaping legacy of beauty at Ole Miss.
- To Chancellor Robert Khayat for having a vision and encouraging mine.
- And, finally, a heartfelt thanks to all my *Weeding Leaders* at Landscape Services. Your insights, your stories, and your *results* inspire me daily.

INTRODUCTION

Many "how to" guides have been written about leading a successful organization … most from a top-down perspective. The problem with this view from the "top" is that, day-to-day, everything below looks less important, less *clear*, and this includes the people, the problems, the opportunities, and the solutions.

This book gives you a glimpse into the lessons I learned from the ground—close up and personal. When I arrived at the University of Mississippi, affectionately known as Ole Miss, as director of Landscape Services in 2000, I came prepared to confront the truth of all those national rankings that listed the state of Mississippi at the bottom. What I discovered at Ole Miss was innate beauty and creativity just waiting for permission to grow.

The University of Mississippi was established in 1848 and now is among the nation's elite research universities. The university is in the highly competitive Southeastern Conference.

Collegiate athletics, especially football, is an exciting part of being at an SEC school. Competition drives the economy, community, and mindset of Ole Miss faculty, staff, and alumni.

Today, the university's main campus encompasses more than 1,000 acres in the beautiful rolling hills of Oxford. Many visitors say they experience a majestic feeling as they walk through the Circle and Grove, and throughout the year, more than 19,000 students, 3,000 faculty and staff, and thousands of football fans enjoy the lushness that is Ole Miss.

When I came on board, it was a different story. Despite being influenced by Frederick Law Olmsted's firm (Olmsted is considered to be the founder of American landscape architecture), Ole Miss' grounds were not prepared as they could have been for recruiting America's finest young minds at the start of the 21st century.

I am not a hired gun, someone who is paid to make changes overnight and move on. When then-Chancellor Robert Khayat interviewed me, he let me know that it would take time and effort to develop the potential of this campus. He understood that a total college campus experience, including an inspiring outdoor environment, was critical to recruiting top-level students, faculty, and staff to the university. He knew that students' (and parents') first impression of the campus would be a major factor in deciding where to go to college.

His goals were big, the landscape budget was small, and so it was critical to look to the people who maintain the landscape to give the university a competitive edge.

Growing "weeders" into "leaders" became the secret sauce that put Ole Miss at the top of several lists. It won four national awards for its beauty, including Most Beautiful Campus by both *The Princeton Review* and *Newsweek*. (We affectionately call these awards our four national championships.)

I studied environments, practices, and methods that allow plants to thrive at Auburn University's School of Horticulture. I learned how to diagnose unhealthy plants and make changes that help plants grow stronger. Learning how to grow thriving plants as well as observing Khayat and other great leaders, I discovered ways to help develop great people and a great team culture.

Ten years into my tenure at Ole Miss, I discovered I was most successful when I began focusing about 20 percent of what I did on the technical aspect of landscaping and 80 percent on staff development. Embracing the latter allowed for a transition in the focus from surviving to thriving. I no longer needed to be the smartest person in the room or have full control of each decision.

As a result, people became more engaged and passionate about their work, and I became more authentic, which, in turn, helped cultivate a new, healthy culture—a culture of greatness producing best practices and solutions.

I learned that having teams participate in the decision-making process has given them greater ownership in what we do. Some of our best ideas come from our front-line staff members. Former U.S. President Ronald Reagan kept a quote on his desk that read, "There is no limit to what you can accomplish if you don't care who gets the credit." Listening to, trusting, and respecting those I work with has paid huge dividends at Ole Miss.

Leadership practices are sacred at any level in any organization. All across the country, in every industry, leadership development that offers the individual employee the opportunity to thrive on both a personal and a professional level is needed. If employees, whether sitting at their desks, standing on a production line, or pulling weeds, understand that their ideas and investment of time, energy, and skill matter, then the *culture of leadership* begins to grow.

Growing Weeders into Leaders takes you through the practical applications of empowering people to experience not only what it means to grow outstanding landscapes but also to grow greatness in themselves and encourage it in others.

The success of developing the nation's most beautiful campus began with Khayat's vision of potential. His passion for making the campus beautiful involved more than just adding a few flowers. His vision allowed me to set into motion a movement in my area that provided the opportunity to develop ideas and techniques used to win my crew's trust. Eventually, it grew into their enthusiastic commitment to our joint vision of cultivating greatness at Ole Miss.

The book relates episodes at Ole Miss Landscape Services and my personal journey and is organized around the path I have taken. My goal in writing this book is to share my experiences with the hope that those in other industries might GROW.

CHAPTER 1

The Story of Thomas

Cultivating Failure

"Failure is simply the opportunity to begin again, this time more intelligently."
—Henry Ford

At 24 years of age, just out of college, Thomas was hired by a large landscaping corporation to manage a high-end resort in Orlando, Florida. He was as green as the grass for which he was responsible, wide-eyed, and a bit overwhelmed; yet, he proved to be talented in the field. In less than a year, he was recruited by another luxury resort in Miami. The resort was rebuilding and hoping to shed its old '70s disco image.

Youngest in his department, Thomas was responsible for overseeing all the landscaping of the magnificent 300-acre resort featuring condominiums, hotels, fine dining, tennis, golf, and a shopping mall.

Yet the resort was also known for its employee theft, highly inefficient production, and challenging labor union. The crew had been left leaderless and on its own to figure out what to do. Territorial turf wars ensued among the staff, club members were getting questionable favors, while some employees could not even be found during the day. Without accountability, everyone did what it took to survive.

Thomas only spoke English in the midst of multilingual workers who talked about him, even while standing right in front of him.

During his naïve, early days of leadership, he was convinced he did not have enough staff to adequately manage all the properties his teams serviced. In a matter of a few months, he increased the size of the crew by 35 percent. He also hired two assistant managers to help provide additional leadership. On paper, it looked good, with plenty of staff, adequate management, and an organizational structure that covered all the areas.

However, the additional staff brought new challenges such as time management, quality control, territorial silo, more people to manage and motivate, more drama, expenses, equipment, uniforms, benefits, more of everything. It was anything but paradise.

To fast-track his lack of plant knowledge in this new tropical climate, Thomas took a night class in horticulture at a nearby community college. He was determined to make the resort property a success and do it quickly. He walked the properties he managed, meeting condo managers, working with vendors, exploring new solutions. Daily, he did one-on-one, in-the-field training with staff. He was always putting out fires, dealing with drama, and constantly creating to-do lists for his staff.

A few months after hiring all the new workers, Thomas got a call from the chief financial officer—a call that brought more bad news. His department was losing money on all the outside contracts. The new hires and additional expenses were busting the budget.

In a rapid response, Thomas worked with leadership and determined that the rates they were charging the customers were too low and needed to be raised. On paper, this looked good to accounting, but the customer base pushed back against the sharp increases. First, one property dropped Thomas' team, then another, and another, until finally seven properties were lost.

With the loss of multiple maintenance contracts, Thomas was faced with yet a new problem, too many staff. The agonizing decision was made to lay off over half his landscape staff.

The day of the layoffs arrived, and Thomas broke the news to each staff member. He would later reflect that it was one of the worst days of his life, knowing these people and their families would be affected by the loss of their jobs. It was a gut-wrenching day preceded and followed by many sleepless nights.

With the downsized staff, Thomas proceeded to work even longer and harder to make the resort properties a success. Willing to jump in and get his hands dirty, he jumped on a tractor from time to time to assist the crews and help foster a higher morale. He had always been taught not to be afraid to get his hands dirty. But in a union environment, where relationships had not been built between management and the workforce, there were misunderstandings.

"You're taking away our jobs by being on the tractor," the union steward complained.

His comment shocked Thomas who was trying to lead by example. He felt betrayed and misunderstood.

Rick Quits

"Do not fear mistakes. You will know failure. Continue to reach out."
—Benjamin Franklin

Rick, a star employee, asked Thomas how he liked the seasonal flower bed that he and his crew had just planted. Thomas was excited and thought they had done a good job, but he did not want them to get overconfident. He praised the work but quickly followed it up with a picky, negative comment about a few plants being imperfectly aligned.

Rick looked disappointed. His shoulders slumped as he looked Thomas in the eye and said, "I quit." He dropped his tools at Thomas' feet and turned and walked away.

As the rest of the crew stared at him, Thomas felt shocked and embarrassed by what had just happened. Rick was known throughout the company as the "go-to guy" on the site, highly talented with many years of experience, and now on Thomas' watch, he had quit.

"Oh no, no, no, no, no," Thomas thought. He wanted to stop Rick, but he let the situation play out.

A day or so later, Rick changed his mind and went back to work. He shared with Thomas what he was hearing not only that day but each day from him.

"It is like we can never please you," he said. "You always have to be critical of our work, and it really hurts our confidence the way you do it."

"Ouch," Thomas thought. This was not easy to hear, so he became defensive but kept silent. But in reflection, he realized Rick was right. As a young manager, Thomas was learning that his words mattered.

Broken

"What we see as failure may actually be progress."
—Dan Miller, Author, "48 Days to the Work You Love"

Late one night after attending his community college horticulture class, Thomas was driving home alone. Two minutes from home, he fell asleep at the wheel. His car slammed into a large tree in the median strip. No one else was hurt, but Thomas was unconscious, and he was rushed to the hospital. Fortunately, he was wearing his seat belt and only suffered minor cuts, a chipped bone in his ankle, and few stitches to the eyebrow.

The next day, a bit groggy, Thomas lay in his hospital bed, staring at the wall, and started to think about work.

After the layoffs, he had received some anonymous hate mail. Doubt about the direction he was going in had begun to worry him. Where was all this going? Was it really worth the price? At times, Thomas felt like it was him versus the crew members, labor against management. He had strived to do the best he could at work, but it was too exhausting.

Thomas recalled the teachings he had learned all his life. He remembered the words of motivational speaker Zig Ziglar: "You can have everything in life you want, if you'll just help enough other people get what they want."

Thomas was beginning to take this to heart. Was there a better way to make others feel respected and appreciated? He realized that nothing was going to change unless he changed first. It took time, but slowly Thomas began to pay more attention to the people with whom he worked. He started providing better training sessions that gave them a sense of purpose at work. He started instilling a sense of pride in the team. In time, the landscape team won several state awards and a national award.

He began to view work through the eyes of his staff members and to tie their tasks back to a larger meaning of why they were there working: to provide for themselves and their families, to being a five-star resort. He reminded them that their work set the first impression, that their role was a vital part of the guest experience. Thomas slowly began to create a team where everyone had a role and every role was important. He was beginning to see the bigger picture.

As you probably have already guessed, the reason I know the story of Thomas so well is because I am Thomas: Jeffery Thomas McManus. As you can see, I made a lot of mistakes. Some may call them failures, but I call them my road to progress.

CHAPTER 2

Cultivating Greatness

Vision Has to Have Meaning

"A rock pile ceases to be a rock pile the moment a single man contemplates it, bearing within him the image of a cathedral."

**—Antoine de Saint-Exupéry, Author,
"The Little Prince"**

sat in University of Mississippi Chancellor Robert C. Khayat's office on a beautiful, sunny day in Oxford. I had never met the chancellor in person and wasn't sure what to expect.

"I want a five-star campus!" he said.

Ah! He knew my background was in hotels and resorts—he was speaking my language! I glanced out the office window, then his eyes caught mine and he nodded. He had a vision for the potential on campus and wanted me to understand. He knew time and neglect had taken their toll on the facilities and landscape of Ole Miss, obscuring the splendor that *could be.* He wanted me on his team, and by the end of that interview, I knew I had found a new home.

My challenge was clear: Make the Ole Miss landscape the best. It would be the secret to accomplishing Khayat's other goals such as recruiting and retaining top students, including student-athletes, and top faculty in the research centers and classrooms.

People want to be associated with winners, and prospective students and their parents, visitors, and faculty and staff candidates would connect quickly with a beautifully landscaped campus.

But reaching that goal was going to be challenging. No one in our department had worked in or knew what it meant to have a five-star property. Most were comfortable where they were. Although the system was dysfunctional, it was a system they knew.

One day, while making my morning rounds, I bumped into the chancellor as he was finishing his early morning walk, and I asked him if I could give him a ride back to his home. He agreed. I asked, "What is the best way to get a vision that people will go along with?" Without hesitation he said, "There are four basic steps you need to follow:

1. Know who you are.
2. Know who you want to be.
3. Get buy-in from everyone.
4. Allow for honest and open feedback and disagreement at any time."

Then he added, "Make the vision big enough to challenge everyone to be the best, to strive for excellence in all they do, to be a leader. **Don't set small goals, and don't get caught up in feeling sorry for yourself as so many people do.** And expect some people to laugh at you. Some people laughed when we first began the process of establishing a Phi Beta Kappa chapter here with the goal of becoming a great American university." He smiled and nodded. "They're not laughing now."

Make Your Vision Stick

"Vision doesn't stick without constant care and attention."
—Andy Stanley, Communicator, Author,
and Pastor

After my interview with Chancellor Khayat, I knew I wanted to help create a top campus and that we needed a great team of people. But I also knew that getting others to have that same desire would be a challenge. Creating the buy-in was going to be the key, and this would take time.

I wanted to pursue setting a vision, so I gathered more insights from leaders such as Andy Stanley and John Maxwell. I was glad to learn that a vision statement can be short. Stanley said eight words or less is enough, and it doesn't have to cover everything you do. It needs to be something everyone can relate to, remember, and repeat.

Our landscape team tried several times to develop a vision statement. Year after year, we hit a road block. **It takes a pecan tree four to eight years to produce pecans. Perhaps it would take our landscape team that long to write the vision statement.** Then, Chris Hardy, one of our landscape student workers, noted while watching our staff working its magic, "We are cultivating greatness." Thus, our vision statement was born.

Growth from Within

"Great men are not born great, they grow great ... "
—Mario Puzo, Author, "The Godfather"

Plants grow quietly and at varying rates. Once we had our vision statement, it was time to go about developing the vision. **And like plants, personal and professional growth happens quietly and at varying speeds.** As the teams moved about campus tending the plants, they started cultivating the greatness within themselves and one another.

Everyone has the potential for greatness. Taking the time to dig around and discover it is the hard part. In Landscape Services, we found the time, and doing so has made us better as a team in our work, and for many of us, in our home lives.

Take Denise Hill for example. One day while walking down the sidewalk, I noticed she was expertly operating a line trimmer. She paused to let me walk by, smiled, nodded, then she went back to work. She was a hardworking, front-line staff member who took a lot of pride in her work. With very little formal training, she energized those around her with her enthusiasm. She stood out among the staff.

After seeing how we were behind in managing the shrubs, flowers, and ground cover, I asked Hill if she would consider tackling this project. She eagerly agreed and began putting her magical touch on the plants. Before long, we added more newly landscaped areas, and her work quickly expanded.

I then asked her if she would consider training a few more people to work with her, and she paused, unsure if she was ready for the challenge of being responsible for the decisions and outcome when one takes on a leadership role. I encouraged her to try and, as expected, she did a wonderful job, and she was promoted to supervisor. She built collaboration and called her work crew "Delta Force" because her team would do things no other team wanted to do.

In time, as my role increased on campus with the addition of the University Airport and then the Ole Miss Golf Course, I needed leaders who could step up to lead our day-to-day operations in Landscape Services. I knew Hill would make a great leader, but when I approached her, she was again hesitant to make the move up. One of the few females on our staff, she would be overseeing her former boss and taking on more responsibilities, but she is a grower at heart. She can grow plants as well as help people develop their potential. She rose to the challenge and is now superintendent of Landscape Services.

Purpose

"The landscaping at Ole Miss makes a huge impact on our recruits and parents."
—Hugh Freeze, head football coach, Ole Miss Rebels

Knowing how important first impressions are for those coming for a college visit elevates our employees' awareness of how important they are when it comes to recruiting top students, faculty, and staff to our campus. According to a Noel-Levitz national research report in 2012 titled "Why Did They Enroll? The Factors Influencing College Choice," 63 percent of four-year, public, first-year students considered appearance of the campus as an important factor when deciding whether to enroll in an institution.

It may sound improbable, but our staff may play a part in helping to cure a disease, sending people into space, or putting the next All-American athlete on the playing field because they help to create that first impression.

Ole Miss Athletics Director Ross Bjork has visited our department on several occasions to help reinforce our impact in recruiting top athletes. Hugh Freeze, head football coach, and Mike Bianco, head baseball coach, have done the same. I knew the vision of cultivating greatness was hitting home with our staff when a team member confessed to the group that he hated putting down pine straw in the shrub beds, but he did it because he might be helping to recruit the next Eli Manning, Patrick Willis, or Dexter McCluster.

David Allen, dean of the School of Pharmacy, and Douglass Sullivan-González, dean of the Sally McDonnell Barksdale Honors College, have visited our team and shared their stories of leadership and expressed the importance of our role in making the job of recruiting the best and brightest students and faculty just a little easier.

These people connect the dots that show our staff members they matter and are making a difference. Yes, we mow grass, trim shrubs, and plant trees, but we also cultivate an environment for others to learn, create, and play while on their way to making a positive change in the world. We are *cultivating greatness*.

CHAPTER 3

Cultivating a Culture

"If you do not change, you can become extinct!"
**—Spencer Johnson, Author, "Who
Moved My Cheese?"**

On May 1, 2000, I introduced myself to members of the newly formed Landscape Services department at Ole Miss. Most of the staff seemed to know already that our new department would now answer directly to both the vice chancellor of finance and administration and the chancellor.

Although some of the former administrators were no longer in charge of this department, most of the challenges were still very much present.

It did not take me long to feel the tension between management and the crews. Daily, I could sense distrust, anger, resentment, confusion, fear, and apathy as I got to know the crew. I wondered why such feelings were so deep, fresh, and evident in the group.

Show You Care

"Putting people before profits is how we've tried to operate from the beginning."
—**S. Truett Cathy, Founder, Chick-fil-A**

Plants grow healthier in the right environment and struggle in an environment that is not conducive to growth. **The leader's behavior and attitude are very important to the environment of an organization.** Whether it is a business or a school, the working environment affects the wellness of the team.

Leaders generally underestimate how much their own behavior affects how people feel about their work. Have you ever gone to your boss's office only to be ignored as he or she stayed on the computer? Maybe you've asked your boss a question, only to be made to feel stupid for asking it.

Mediocre leaders underestimate the value of respecting people with whom they work. It can be the easiest thing to stop what you're doing and simply smile and acknowledge people as you encounter them.

It didn't take long to see how the former landscape leadership affected the department negatively. I didn't realize how toxic the landscape culture was before I was hired.

Putting people down, showing them little or no respect for what they do or who they are will undermine employees' trust in and respect for a leader.

Getting employees to be productive and passionate about what they do takes positive leadership. Great leaders find ways to connect with their people, respect them, serve them, and make them successful. Poor leaders use their position to keep people in line rather than motivate them.

When I observed Chancellor Khayat as he walked the campus in the mornings, he often shook people's hands, smiled, waved, or stopped to ask questions. I knew he was sincere when I watched custodial staff members' faces "light up" and wave across campus when they saw him. That told me they respected him, felt comfortable to approach him, and were glad to see him. **People don't care how much you know until they know how much you care.**

Keep on Plowing

"Before anyone is willing to follow you – or any other leader – he or she wants to know that you are honest, forward-looking, inspiring, and competent."
—Kouzes & Posner, The Leadership Challenge

I believed there was nowhere to go but up with the Landscape Services department, but I was wrong. At times, things got worse, much worse. It was part of the process of getting better, dealing with years of deep-rooted bad performances and lack of good mid-level leadership. I understand why new owners of struggling companies immediately let the leadership go when they take over. It's a lot simpler to immediately let everyone go and start all over, but that option was never on the table.

I met some strong-rooted resistance to change, but I didn't stop cultivating it. I had to focus on the small wins as they came to keep me motivated. Those who didn't want to embrace the new direction either left our organization or were held accountable. Several chose to make progress a real challenge. I often heard, "That is not the way we do it here," or "We always do it like this."

In farming terms, **leaders need to keep plowing and breaking up the hard soil so the new seeds they plant can take root and grow deep.** That's what I did, so in time, some of the staff started sensing a change.

I learned early to seek wisdom from others, especially when it came to personnel matters. I've always valued and relied on the counsel of those in the Human Resources department. I view them as a strong partner in achieving success. I learned early to listen and do what they said to resolve tough challenges with our hard cases. At times they seem to slow us down, but in the big picture HR is there to assist and create a good workplace.

In those early days, it was painful to observe what little direction, scheduling, accountability, or positive encouragement was taking place in the department. Front-line leaders were left to figure out most every aspect of their grounds work on the 1,000-acre campus.

It was a highly reactive schedule, going from one fire to the next. Staff members were stressed and kept to themselves. In many tasks, they were self-taught. Without standards, consistency was lacking in the look of the grounds, the way the equipment was serviced, and pretty much everything else.

I wished at times I could snap my fingers and it would all be fixed, but it wasn't going to be that simple. In our university system, you may have issues with an employee, but it takes continued documentation and multiple warnings to terminate someone in most cases. The process is much the same for large corporations. It is a process put in place to ensure policies are adhered to and people are treated fairly.

I needed to make some real changes both to the campus grounds and in the personnel, and knew I had to earn the staff's trust. This is true in any industry. In Stephen A. Covey's book *The Speed of Trust*, he explains that work speed increases when there is high trust and decreases when there is low trust.

Having high levels of trust allows organizations to do more with less. Fewer rules and policies exist with high levels of trust. People who trust are more willing to collaborate, share, and engage in their work.

I made sure if I said something, I stood by it. I didn't want to make empty promises. In my previous job, I mistakenly gave a few raises the first year I was there. This had a negative effect on others as it rippled through the crew and started a revolving door of special requests for everyone.

At Ole Miss, I wanted to listen and include team members in the process. I wanted a culture that was not driven by excuses, raises, retirement plans, or other employee benefits. I didn't get caught in the short-term incentives that don't motivate staff long term.

Think Like an Investor

"A leadership culture is one where everyone thinks like an owner, a CEO or a managing director. It's one where everyone is entrepreneurial and proactive."
—Robin S. Sharma, Canadian Author & Leadership Speaker

Prior to my arrival to Ole Miss, alumnus Larry Martindale and his wife, Susan, along with others, had graciously invested extensively in the landscaping beautification campaign project spearheaded by Chancellor Khayat. An outside landscape contractor was brought in to do the new beautification work around a few buildings, but as quickly as the projects were completed, problems arose, highly visual ones.

When the Martindales visited campus to see the return on their investment, they were troubled by the new plants that had died, the overgrown weeds, and the lack of care and maintenance.

Finger pointing took place at the mid-management level with lots of hurt feelings to go around, but credit Khayat for being solution-oriented as he quickly reached out to Auburn horticulture professor Harry Ponder for assistance, who in turn recommended me.

Khayat told me how Larry Martindale, who was part owner of the Ritz-Carlton Hotel and Resorts, said that the price of any property is set at the front entrance. I believe that is true. A property's appearance says a lot about the leadership and value placed on the campus or any organization. It tells parents a lot about how we value their children. Studies show clean, well-landscaped areas are safer. What parent doesn't want that?

Find Hidden Leaders

"The growth and development of people is the highest calling of leadership."
—Harvey Firestone, Founder, Firestone Tire and Rubber Company

During my first few months at Ole Miss, I asked lots of questions. I constantly assessed and took inventory of what kind of people, plants, and support I had on campus. I tried to understand what was happening before I made any changes. Years later, I watched Dan Jones, M.D., who succeeded Khayat as chancellor, do this better than I did.

His first year as chancellor, he was constantly observing and asking questions to understand and evaluate the organization. He confirmed the importance of understanding your culture, your assets, and getting insights before making changes.

However, our situations differed on one major point. Chancellor Jones took over an organization that was on an upward trajectory. When I started in my department, it was just the opposite. It was spiraling downward.

My first months, I was constantly being told by some in landscaping that we didn't have enough people to do the job. We didn't have enough equipment or money, the campus was too big, and the chancellor's expectations were unrealistic.

The landscape operating system was set up to be reactive not proactive. Employees got work orders each morning to deal with complaints and work requests. I was surprised that our department was getting work orders to mow the lawn, trim the shrubs, and other routine maintenance items on campus. Why were we waiting for work orders to do work when we should be doing this as part of our daily schedule? "That is just the way we do it," was a common answer.

Inefficient practices such as riding to a location only to briefly work and then drive back to the shop to take a scheduled break were common. I constantly saw one staff member looking into the dumpsters on campus. I thought he had been put in charge of checking them as much time as he spent looking in them each day. When I asked what he was doing, he sheepishly admitted he was looking for "treasures" that he could take home. It was clearer why the chancellor was frustrated with the lack of production.

In the midst of this chaos, I found many staff members who were looking for a better place to work. Several staff members had quit and others said they had been ready to quit, but they wanted to see if things changed with new leadership. These staff members would be key to cultivating a new, dynamic culture. No one person creates an incredible team. It takes many who are committed. Great leaders look to build collaboration.

Days of riding or walking with the staff allowed me a chance to get to know our team and see if we had any hidden talent among our staff. **If you're paying attention, those leaders you want and need may be there.** Sometimes they're like seedlings being overshadowed by a large oak. A wise leader will nurture, develop, and transplant those good seedlings so they can grow stronger.

Take Inventory

"First thing, take an inventory."
—Harry Ponder, horticulture professor,
Auburn University

Harry Ponder and my dad encouraged me during my first week of work at Ole Miss to take a good inventory of what was on site. Ponder focused on the plant materials, and my dad focused on the people and equipment. I thought that was good advice and wish I had taken more photographs of the sites before we started changing them so I could have before-and-after photos.

I knew going in, we were going to need additional equipment. No one in Landscape Services was overseeing irrigation or weed control, and very little if any time was given to managing the shrubs and trees on campus. Almost all of the crew's time was spent on mowing weeds and grass.

The shop area, where the crew met in the mornings and at lunch, was a hazardous collection of chemicals, scattered parts, bags of fertilizer, unused bins, and piled-up messes. In the middle of this mess, staff members were supposed to figure out where to eat, fix equipment, sharpen mower blades, and keep their work materials. It was chaos behind peeling-paint double doors that read "GROUNDS."

It was easy to see why so many people had quit work. I found this same scenario in every "Grounds" storage area I visited. How could I ask for equipment when what we had was not being maintained, pride in ownership didn't exist, and no one trusted that if we got something new we would take care of it? It was a mess that seem to attract more and more chaos the bigger it got. No one cared, and no one was responsible.

Share Core Values

"We make a living by what we get, we make a life by what we give."
—Winston Churchill

Changing the culture started slow like planting seeds. It started by sharing my core values many times. Be solution oriented, work smarter not harder, have an eye for detail, set the example, be the best of the best. These simple phrases helped move us down the path to changing the mindset.

When starting out, let people know your core values, write them down, and post them. It helps people to identify who you are and what you stand for. I never said, "Work hard" or "Do your job right." I said, "Let's be the best of the best."

Core values matter in an organization if you want to do more than survive to retirement. Letting people know your values is not a one-and-done exercise. The better you get at practicing them, the better the organization becomes.

We have all seen managers who never discuss or introduce core values to their organization. They simply surrender to the culture they are in charge of, letting it toss them and the organization to and fro. It takes courage to continue to be positive and work for greater change, to embrace the deeper meaning of what you do.

When I first asked supervisors if there was a better way to do things, I got a lot of blank stares. I could tell some of the staff didn't feel comfortable in conversation and did not fully trust this approach. Their experience told them to keep their mouths shut and heads down, and that their opinions didn't matter. Do what you're told.

To help develop knowledge, understanding, and new standards, I started doing technical training classes to teach the landscape crew about best practices. We did pruning classes, as well as classes on how to run and maintain equipment. Much of this training was new to our staff members, who were highly attentive. People who wanted to do a good job embraced the standards and excelled in their work.

When I asked why the mowers kept breaking down, I was told, "We don't have time to service them."

Mowers are the workhorses of the modern-day campus landscape. They are used to mow grass in the summer, mulch leaves in the fall, and remove snow in the winter. When a mower breaks down, efficiency goes down. More work is placed on the crews, which delays production.

In time, we established preventive maintenance on each mower prior to and after each operation in the field. The result was that our mower repair costs dropped overnight. Air filters were cleaned, grease points greased, debris removed. Instead of running equipment until it stopped and dropped, staff members learned to be proactive and service it every day.

Core values helped us focus on where we were going as a group.

Work Smarter, Not Harder

"Working smart means wringing maximum production from your work schedule. It's coming up with new ideas to bring that about."
—Robert Terson, Sales Professional and Entrepreneur

"Work smarter, not harder" has become routine in Landscape Services. For example, our team would receive a work order requesting the removal of a large tree limb obstructing a walkway. A crew member would be lifted up in a front-end loader tractor with a chainsaw in hand and cut the limb off. It was effective but not the safest way to do the task.

We purchased a tool to do this task in a smarter way. A high-reaching pole saw for less than $100 got the job done much safer and a bit quicker, and the staff appreciated it.

It wasn't long before someone spotted gas pole chainsaws in a supply catalog. For about $750, we increased production and trimmed more tree limbs than with the manual pole saws. Our team never got in a tractor bucket again to trim limbs.

Details Matter

"It's the little details that are vital. Little things make big things happen."
—John Wooden

I first learned to have an eye for detail when I started working at the Grand Cypress Resort in Orlando right out of college. Jamie Boynton, my boss with then Quant-Aires Enterprise, a contracting firm, spent a lot of time showing me what an eye for detail looked like in landscaping.

He taught me to look for straight edging patterns at 90 degrees, how lawns transition seamlessly between line trimmers and mowers where no one can notice the difference in mowing heights. He continued to make sure I was looking daily for things like weed-free shrub beds and clean, manicured flower beds that showed a high level of attention and detail.

This training permanently gave me a high standard, and I have a hard time letting go of it. I have to turn off the eye for detail when I go on vacation so I don't start making lists in my head of what needs to be done.

Too much mulch piled up on the base of plants, insect damage, yellowing plants, dead plants, fire ant mounds, uneven bed lines, hedges sheared instead of selectively pruned, the list goes on. These are the little details that matter in the big picture, especially if you want to have championship results.

As Boynton taught me about having an eye for detail, he encouraged me to walk the site daily with the people who maintained it, to teach them to have an eye for detail.

I learned to pause, go inside the hotel, and observe what the guest sees. What does the landscaping look like as a first-time visitor? You may have an excuse for why the landscape looks bad, but first-time visitors do not know that. They only see it and make judgments.

Now Landscape Services staff learns about having an eye for detail. When staff members embrace this concept, they want the campus to live up to a high standard. It's fun hearing staff comment on things they see on and off our campus.

Some staff and I took trips to several major SEC campuses. On one campus, the first thing our staff noticed was all the grass clippings on the sidewalk in front of the campus's iconic building. A few hours later, as we were touring around with the campus landscape manager, the grass clippings were still scattered on the sidewalk and clumped up on the lawn.

The manager commented on how tall the grass had grown due to all the rain and that the landscape staff was way behind on mowing. It was tough on him, it looked bad, but we understood, it happens.

After we finished our tour and said our goodbyes to the campus landscape manager, we piled into our van and started our drive to the next location. It didn't take long before we started talking about those grass clippings.

That one four-hour tour was worth 100 hours of training. Because most of the staff in the van had never been to that campus before, it truly was their first impression. Even today, years after that tour, those staff members talk about those grass clippings making a huge mess on that campus. First impressions matter.

It is easy to judge another group's property and to be critical, but if you think that is what I am saying, then you miss the point. The win for us was our people were developing an eye for detail; they saw how important first impressions are and how they would have done it differently. By developing an eye for detail, they were engaged in seeing the problems and finding solutions.

Create Picture-Perfect Moments

"You don't take a photograph, you make it."
—Ansel Adams, American Photographer

Boynton taught me another great lesson about large property management. Always create areas where people want to take photos. People appreciate those unique spaces, and they want to take that memory home with them. Many companies and schools have this figured out. In marketing terms, creating iconic photo areas helps reinforce the brand to consumers.

Be the Best of the Best

"Be a yardstick of quality. Some people aren't used to an environment where excellence is expected."
—Steve Jobs

The first few years, it was obvious the department was in spiral decline, an arborist's term we use when a tree is dying little by little each year. It is hard if not impossible to get a tree out of spiral decline. Fortunately, our department was able to come out of it.

One of the things a leader can do to make this happen is to paint a better picture for the team to see and follow. I started painting a verbal picture of where we were going. I'd say, "We want to be the best of the best."

Each time I said this, I would define it. "We want to be the best of the best in our industry, one of the best-looking colleges in the United States. … We want to be the best of the best, just like Disney World is to Florida and the resort business. … We want to be the best in the SEC and the country." In time, I heard our staff repeat it, "We want to be the best of the best." It was simple, to the point, and it gave us a future. We were cultivating a culture of shared values.

CHAPTER 4

Low-Hanging Fruit

Identify Quick Wins

"Talent wins games, but teamwork and intelligence wins championships."
—Michael Jordan

Landscape Services needed some quick wins, some low-hanging fruit if you will. **As with most endeavors, when you can build on the small wins, it helps lead to bigger**

wins. In football, coaches want small wins such as first downs, field position, rushing and passing yards, and a defense that takes the ball away. In most cases, enough small wins lead to winning the game, having a winning season, and winning the championship.

I needed some first downs, and I didn't have to look far. I knew the Grove was a key area of concern for Chancellor Khayat and a cherished place at Ole Miss. I focused on one key directive in this area in hopes of seeing quick improvement. Not all change is obvious, but my hope was this one would be.

The limbs on many of the trees in the Grove were too low to walk under without ducking. It was hard to appreciate the magnificent view through the Grove because the limbs obstructed it. One crew member proudly said that trees in the Grove were never pruned. Based on the way the trees looked, I believed him.

One of the crew's challenges was a lack of proper pruning tools. Of course, if you're not going to prune any trees, then it makes sense not to have any tree-pruning tools. We purchased a few extension pole saws and did some tree-pruning training classes with the staff, and then turned them loose in the Grove.

Khayat noticed the change immediately, as well as others on campus. Our landscaping staff received comments about the big improvement. Not only could people walk through the

Grove without ducking but also the mower operators were no longer getting hit in the face with the limbs. It was just like getting a first down in football.

Opportunity

"Your big opportunity may be right where you are now."
—Napoleon Hill, American Author

The landscape staff members had experienced lots of frustrating problems before I arrived, and one of them was their uniforms were outdated, in bad shape, and uncomfortable to wear outdoors. The staff also complained that the uniforms were not being laundered correctly.

In dealing with the issue, the goal was to get everyone to wear the same professional level of dress. As their leader, I could simply tell the crews to wear the uniforms and leave it at that, but I wanted our team to take pride in wearing them, not to feel like they were being made to wear them.

Our landscape team decided to drop the laundry service, purchase its own fitted uniforms, and that each employee would be responsible for laundering and caring for his or her own uniform.

When leaders ignore issues important to staff, they communicate that they don't care. **Leaders show they care when they listen and then do what they can to find solutions.**

At the time, some told me I was wasting my time and "chasing squirrels" on such things that I couldn't change. The easy thing to do is to lie down and give in to the situation and let it defeat us. In football, coaches will risk 4th and 1 to change the game and go for the win. **Opportunities often come dressed as problems and challenges.** The uniform issue was a good way to get our staff to collaborate in coming up with alternative solutions.

Be Resourceful

"Three rules of work: Out of clutter find simplicity; from discord find harmony; In the middle of difficulty lies opportunity."
—Albert Einstein

The staff was taking 10 days to mow the entire campus lawn area when I first arrived. A year or so before I got there, an expert had been hired by Physical Plant to figure out how to make the landscape areas more efficient. The campus was to be mowed in four days with one day left in the week left to do pruning, flowers, and odds and ends. Because it was taking the staff 10 days to finish mowing, the other items were not completed.

It didn't take long to see some major flaws in the process. For example, the mower operations were slower than they needed to be. Each day, the mower operators were having to work around the picnic tables, benches, trash cans, light poles, bollards, trees, and signage.

In an ideal setting, mowers should sweep in and out of lawn areas with no backing up, limited turning, and very little stopping. It was time to work smarter, not harder.

After meeting with crews in the field, we determined if there was a way to move an object, such as a trash can, sign, or bench, we moved it or eliminated it, and trash cans were strategically put in beds where there was no grass.

Mowing crews found ways to keep from backing up and having to make multiple turns and slow operating moves to weave through an area. The simplest way was to eliminate 90 degree turns by changing to gentle "sweeping" turns in our mowing areas. Our operators embraced the changes and made them successful.

We were able to add pine straw in areas to eliminate the turf in hard-to-reach areas. This not only increased efficiency but also gave the campus a much-needed boost in beauty. In many areas under trees, shade was not allowing the turf to grow, leaving patches of weeds and bare soil exposed. These areas still needed to be mowed to control the weeds, but they were an eyesore. The use of pine straw covered up these areas, which eliminated unnecessary mowing.

The campus landscape was starting to have areas of well-defined turf and mulch. It "popped," and people were taking notice. Best of all, it was decreasing our mowing times.

It was exciting to see the staff embrace making changes in the field. As with any management change, we lost several employees during the months after I arrived. I chose not to hire anyone back in those vacant positions until I could figure out what we were doing and get the place organized.

We were becoming more efficient, even with the loss of seven full-time staff over the first year, and in just a few months we were mowing the campus in fewer than 10 days. We had 24 full-time employees and maintained this level of staff for two years before we refilled any positions.

Another step we took was to work to eliminate aggressive, fast-growing weeds such as dallisgrass. When I started work, mowing crews often would mow their zone on Monday, and by Thursday the weeds had already reached noticeable mowing height. These tall, unsightly weeds would generate work orders for the landscape staff to come and mow the same zone again.

By hiring a qualified turf expert, David Jumper, we were able to put a good weed prevention program in place. This made us much more efficient because we mowed less, thus using less labor and fuel. We were able to deploy staff to other projects.

Jumper's lead-by-example work ethic made it easy years later to promote him to oversee the golf course operations at Ole Miss. When it came to turf management, he allowed us to "work smarter, not harder."

Remove Obstacles

"Imagination has a great deal to do with winning."
—Mike Krzyzewski, Head Basketball
Coach, Duke University

Remove every obstacle you can to make your team successful. We used to start work at 7:30 a.m. on campus. It was too late in the morning to be highly productive before students, faculty, and staff arrived. The start time was changed to 6 a.m., and our team embraced the change. It made their workday more productive, and they got to go home earlier. Give them the tools they need, and develop systems to keep up with them. Not having tools and equipment is a big morale killer.

Senseless busy work also kills morale. We had every supervisor doing his or her time reports on one computer in the office. It was a big bottleneck and unproductive use of time. One administrator took over the task and freed up everyone to be outside. Teams see your core values on display when you help them work smarter not harder.

We discovered early that no matter how we landscaped next to a building, someone needed to have access to the space right up next to the building foundation. It seemed over and over again our plants were getting stepped on, broken, and we were losing the plants.

We took action by constantly monitoring and seeing what was going on. Window washing, digging, sealing, painting, cleaning, and general maintenance put staff in direct conflict with our plants. At first we thought that we could manage this with conversations and working with departments to keep the plants from being damaged, but soon we realized this was too big of a task that happened too often by people we did not see all times of the day. The campus was too big and spread out.

We decided to revisit the way we landscaped and where we could eliminate the plants up next to the building foundation. A 10-foot buffer off the building before we plant dropped conflicting occurrences and raised morale for all involved, especially our staff. Eliminating hassles for the team is leading by example.

Do It Right for Long-term Success

"Winning is not a sometime thing; it's an all the time thing. You don't win once in a while... you don't do things right once in a while ... you do them right all the time. Winning is habit."
—Vince Lombardi

As our crews were becoming more efficient in the field, we were still being hampered by major equipment breakage and down time. Three new mowers had been ordered well before I had been hired and were a welcome asset. However, neither a preventive maintenance program nor a professional mechanic to service and repair the mowers was in place.

The first person who had been appointed "shade tree mechanic" of the shop asked me if he could purchase a claw hammer. I mistakenly thought he was going to use the hammer to build some much-needed shelving in the shop, which is something we had discussed once before. It was a $16 purchase, so I didn't ask why he needed it.

I soon discovered that he used the hammer to work on the brakes of one of the new mowers. That claw hammer repair job went bad and ended up costing us over $800, with the mower being out of service for two months.

It was actually a blessing in disguise because it validated what position we needed next – a mechanic.

Because we were able to show the university administrators some positive changes in the campus appearance in a short time, while reducing labor, they approved the decision to hire a full-time mechanic.

After creating the mechanic position, we were fortunate to attract David Hodge, a former business owner and certified General Motors mechanic. Hodge often built his own tools to solve challenges. He transformed our little back-of-the-house shop into a highly respected repair center on campus. He was able to teach landscaping staff little tricks to keep equipment running and in tip-top shape.

He would notice trends, log repairs, and help us identify preventable problems. His tracking was able to alert us that we were getting a steady stream of backpack blowers that needed repaired for the same issue. He noticed our staff members would only wear one strap of a backpack blower, leaving the unit to sit at a slight angle across the back, causing mechanical problems.

Hodge convinced them to wear both straps to get better and longer use of the blowers.

Highly qualified, team-oriented staff is a key component of a championship system. Today, new hires in our department take classes to learn how to think efficiently and productively like Hodge. It has become the new normal for us.

Communicate

"The single biggest problem in communication is the illusion that it has taken place."
—George Bernard Shaw

Weekly department meetings became the new norm to train, discuss professionalism, get feedback, and get on the same page. Once a week, we discussed our standards, shared where we were going, and validated people as important to the organization. The early fruit was that people were open to becoming the best. The long-range fruit was in developing leaders who one day would lead the meetings, train, and develop themselves as well as others.

To further create better communication, I tried to make the organization as flat as possible, meaning I wanted to have direct access to everyone on our team and them to me. I didn't want to create this layer of being unapproachable due to the chain of command. The best way I did this was to be among the teams as they worked each day. I hung around the break room and talked to them at the end of the day.

I would invite a staff member to take a drive in the golf cart and look at something together, which was low pressure, no eye contact. It's a good way just to enjoy getting to know someone and get his or her perspective.

Be real, be approachable, and listen.

Take Pride in the Workplace

"Artists are people with a genius for finding a new answer, a new connection, or a new way of getting things done. That could be you."
—Seth Godin, American Author and Entrepreneur

It was time to tackle the cluttered landscape shop area. We could gain valuable time every day by being organized in our shop. Key people in our department started figuring out ways to improve it. We found some space in a nearby warehouse and decided we needed to move items that we didn't use much there.

The clutter was recycled, trashed, stored, or organized for later use. In time we were able to convince the paint shop to give us some old surplus paint, and on a rainy day, we applied fresh, bright paint on the clammy concrete walls in our shop. **Staff immediately liked the change and smiled about it.**

We had so much room now, we made a break room, a mechanic's bay, and the storage space we needed. The back of the house, the Landscape Services shop, had become a point of pride for our staff. The best part is it cost us very little and made us feel good about our work space.

CHAPTER 5

Cultivating Greatness through Training

"If you think that training and development are the exclusive role of human resources or some other department and that you are too busy to bother with them, you might want to rethink what it means to be a leader."

—Lee Cockerell, former executive vice president, operations, Walt Disney World Resort

After a few years of figuring out our standards and systems, we thought we were pretty good at what we did, but we also saw the inconsistency in our own production and services. One crew did a work task one way, and another crew did it another way.

Landscape University (or Landscape U) is an internal training and development system for staff members. It allows us to systemize, track, and develop our training thoroughly, efficiently, and intentionally.

Landscape U focuses on two core modules: technical training and leadership development. Both are critical to building highly motivated teams that seek solutions and develop a positive work culture.

The program has increased the confidence of the team because it gives everyone consistent training and accountability using the standards we had developed together. The last several years, I have had the privilege to share with other organizations from varied industries how to create their own grassroots training program.

One monthly class called "Leader to Leader" features leaders from all walks of life who challenge class participants to raise their thinking to that of a leader. The discussions allow them to recognize their individual talents and ways to develop them.

The argument against the Leader to Leader class is a lack of time. It does take time. Sharpening your mower blades takes time too, but you do it to make a better cut, to ward off wear on the mower, and it speeds up the process by eliminating the double cut on the lawn.

The best way to create a healthy lawn is to grow healthy grass. It takes good food, water, and sunlight. A healthy environment allows the growth of good turf grass and doesn't allow weeds to grow. It takes being intentional in scheduling and organizing.

Today, we are not a perfect group, we still have issues, but we have a strong, healthy culture of staff members leading themselves and others, and the issues just aren't as many or nearly on the same scale. Staff members will reach out to help other staff members who are struggling. It is like having everyone in the same boat, rowing together to get to the same destination. People know when, where, how, and why we are going there.

Why Landscape University?

"Job training empowers people to realize their dreams and improve their lives."
—Sylvia Mathews Burwell, American Executive and the 22nd United States Secretary of Health and Human Services

The Ole Miss football game ended around 6 p.m. No. 1 Alabama had just been upset by the then No. 4 Ole Miss football team. After the game, students rushed the field to celebrate and take down the goalpost. It was a satisfying feeling for the Ole Miss faithful to finally beat Alabama in a game that mattered.

That beautiful crisp fall day had started with ESPN GameDay in the Grove and an appearance by pop star Katy Perry. Many fans had come to the Grove early Saturday morning in hopes of being on TV. The No. 1 team in the nation playing the No. 4 team brought in a larger than normal crowd to the campus.

Our landscaping team had set out some 2,000 waste receptacles and more than 300 recycling bins, and passed out hundreds of garbage bags to help manage the waste generated by game day. Most home football games generate 60-70 tons of waste and recyclables. This game set a record of 90 tons. That is a lot of waste dispersed in a 10-acre area on campus.

Our staff and the student groups we hired arrived at midnight that night to do their magic. Three hours later, the 90 tons of scattered waste had been neatly contained.

One newcomer to campus commented, "I left here last night, and the Grove was in such a mess. This morning, I drove on campus and was shocked to see all the trash is gone, I mean really gone."

Training, preparation, and organization go a long way in creating the unique experience of visiting campus and tailgating in the Grove. Our staff knows that prospective students visit our campus almost every day and may decide in the first few minutes whether to attend the university, based on the appearance of the campus. Getting the Grove and campus back in top condition is one of the priorities of our organization. This is part of our culture, our training, and now it is a part of who we are.

Training is so much easier to do when you have the right players on the team, but even when the team is not filled with the exact players you want, start training anyway, and never stop.

Training has helped fill in the gaps where staff members were lacking in skills and knowledge. It is not a cure-all, but it helps set up a culture of learning and growth. The key to training is to be consistent, relevant, and accountable. This is important as organizations are constantly faced with change and adapting new ways of doing things. As a leader, it is important to give your team the best training, tools, and educational experience to set them up for success.

Great leaders know how to delegate and empower those with whom they work. Doing all the work yourself leads to a dead-end road of frustration and burnout. It is a process of letting go, but when people are properly trained and coached, it becomes a very transforming and successful experience.

It involves an upfront cost of time and energy that is intimidating. It is much easier to stay busy doing your work than to invest in making the process better and more efficient. It is easier in the short term to do it yourself than to train, delegate, and inspect the work. It just is. But long term, if you ever want to get to the next level of where you want your organization, you will need to train your employees and keep training them.

We see this in great organizations that continue to produce high quality work year after year. All the top service-driven companies had a set training program they used: Disney, the Ritz-Carlton, the military.

No paycheck or personal success will ever top the satisfaction of seeing the people you lead achieve new heights and aspirations. Creating a vehicle that allows people to understand their direction and why they are important to the organization makes them a part of something bigger. Watching our people deal with challenges and find solutions to problems is very satisfying.

When our team feels empowered to take the Landscape U system and use it, it increases efficiencies and decreases costs. The beauty of the system is that while one person may champion a solution to an issue, Landscape U allows all the staff in the department to give their input. This has dramatically increased the buy-in to our training. It gives people a voice in what they are doing.

I must warn you, however, that in growing weeders to leaders, you must be willing to let others get the credit for the work and be there to encourage them.

Also, know that if you're not willing to hear contrary input and be open to what your team is saying, you will be just wasting your time. **Mediocre leaders will not tolerate "negative" input to their world and will look for ways to eliminate these voices from their area.** I have seen weak leaders isolate great staff members because they disagreed with him or her. Developing leadership in people is not about everyone following and being a yes man or woman. It is about developing a vision, mission, and core values to live by and help the organization succeed.

Most people know how to meet job expectations. Many managers are fine with that, and many are elated to get the minimum amount of work done. But, great leaders and great organizations don't stop at just meeting the requirement, they go beyond that.

Leaders reach far beyond the minimum requirements and excel in excellence daily. They find ways to invest in themselves, others, and what they do. You find them going the extra mile without anyone asking them to do it. You find in many a passion for what they do.

While hosting a conference on the Ole Miss campus, "How to Create Your Own Landscape University," it appeared some folks just came to figure out a way "not" to do what we were teaching and seemed happy to make excuses.

More encouragingly, some people looked at the challenges and figured out how this new information could work for them; how they could modify it, run it, and benefit from it. It is no surprise they are the ones who usually are doing well in other areas. **They are solution focused, not excuse focused.**

Some people call developing people a "soft skill." I dislike that term because it sounds weak. Developing people is anything but weak. It is how to build champions, leaders, and people with a purpose. There is nothing "soft" about it. I believe that is why most neglect to try it. It takes courage and grit to want the best for the organization by way of development.

Results of Training

"Before you are a leader, success is all about growing yourself. When you become a leader, success is all about growing others."
—Jack Welch, Former CEO, General Electric

Staff development in our area has made many of our staff friendlier, stronger, and much more efficient. A front-line groundskeeper, I'll call him Stan, took the teachings he had heard in our Leader to Leader development class to heart. For many years, he has been a faithful and hardworking member of our team.

Dependable and agreeable, he decided he wanted to do more with his life. One day I received an email from someone on campus saying what a great job Stan had done over the weekend at the entrepreneur competition conference on campus. Stan had not only entered the contest, but he also had placed in the top 10 out of 50.

Six months before the conference, Stan had signed up and enrolled in weeklong school in St. Louis to become an auctioneer. Challenged to find consistent, paying auctioneer gigs, he decided he would pitch a business idea to see if he could get prospective investors to help him start a local car auction, something he could do each week. The courage to follow his dream was something I was proud to see.

Later, Stan was sidelined by a brain tumor. It slowed him down but didn't stop him. He soon recovered and was back at work, happier than ever. Stan hasn't yet had that chance to start the local auction, but he is in the game to follow his dream. He said the Leader to Leader classes opened his eyes to his potential and showed him he could "do more than just take up space in life."

Another employee took a job in another department on campus, which paid more than his job in our department. When he saw the job opening, this employee, I will call him Jerome, let me know he was considering applying for it. He knew I would not retaliate against him or sabotage his efforts by giving him a bad reference.

Jerome came to me several times as he struggled with whether or not to apply for the job. We talked about the pros and cons of taking the new job. Some people argue that if you train people, they just leave for better jobs. Why waste the time training only to see them leave? But I don't think training employees is a waste of time.

Jerome told me during his exit interview that it was our Leader to Leader classes that gave him the confidence to apply for the new job. I hated to lose him, but it was time for him to apply what he learned to other areas.

He said the Leader to Leader classes also helped him at home, making him think through some things and get organized and focused. He even said the classes helped improve his marriage.

"What's worse than training your people and losing them?
Not training them and keeping them."
—John C. Maxwell, "The 360 Degree
Leader: Developing Your Influence from
Anywhere in the Organization"

Don't wait for Human Resources or anyone else to invest in your team, or you will miss a great opportunity to do something really great. There is no greater job satisfaction than to see the people you are working with achieve their professional and personal aspirations. It takes you and them to new level of maturity and understanding.

CHAPTER 6

Everyone Is a Leader

"Leaders don't create followers, they create more leaders."
—Tom Peters, Co-Author, "In Search of Excellence"

At one Monday morning meeting, I asked the staff members to raise their hands if they considered themselves leaders. Only a few raised or semi-raised their hands. I also interviewed a dozen or so staff members one-on-one, posing the same question.

A few thought they might be leaders if they had the most experience at a task. Others said they were leaders if their supervisor told them they were. Some said flat out, "I am not a leader. I don't make decisions, I am not in charge, and I don't tell others what to do."

It was enlightening to hear their responses. I had considered everyone on our team to be a leader but realized I had never told them.

I believe you lead one person every day, yourself. You may not have the title, but you still lead yourself. People who go to work extremely moody or emotional can influence other co-workers negatively. Oppositely, people who smile, clock in on time, and are pleasant to work with have a positive influence on everyone. All of us choose how we respond to our circumstances, and that choice affects others.

Titles Don't Make You a Leader

"Leadership is not about titles, positions or flowcharts. It is about one life influencing another."
—John Maxwell, Author and Speaker

A leadership title will get you respect to your face, but you have to earn it to your back. You will earn respect with or without a title by the way you handle yourself and treat others. Being trustworthy and treating people with respect will go a long way toward earning the admiration of those with whom you work.

Those in leadership positions who expect people to "do what I say and not what I do" find they lose influence with those they lead. They lose credibility when they say one thing and do another. It's very hard to trust that type of "leader."

Why Develop Leaders?

"People want guidance, not rhetoric; they need to know what the plan of action is and how it will be implemented. They want to be given responsibility to help solve the problem and the authority to act on it."
—Howard Schultz, Starbucks

Plants respond well to being tended to and nurtured along the way. We are not much different. Championship programs don't happen by accident. **You have to know what you want, plant it, water it, and nurture it.** You have to spend time cultivating that growth. If not, other things start growing that you didn't plant or want.

If you are a leader of an organization, you need a team culture that is empowered with high standards, professionalism, knowledge, and passion to do work with excellence. You need proactive problem solvers who work smarter not harder and by all means want to be the best of the best.

You don't need warm bodies who go through the motions of having a job. You need people who want to do something great with their lives and who are not just there to get a pension in 25 years. Leadership training gives you a great platform to develop these positive qualities.

Plant Seeds of Leadership

"Think twice before you speak, because your words and influence will plant the seed of either success or failure in the mind of another."
—Napoleon Hill, Author, "Think and Grow Rich"

If you want to grow oak trees, you need to be sure you plant oak trees, not maple trees. Once you plant oak trees, you need to be familiar with oak trees' growth needs and help nurture that growth environment. These laws of nature apply to teams too. If you want to develop a strong team of leaders that wants to do incredible work, then you need to nurture that environment. Healthy work environments don't happen by accident. They have to be grown intentionally.

Environment Matters

"The first step toward success is taken when you refuse to be a captive of the environment in which you first find yourself."
—**Mark Caine, American Author**

A leader works at cultivating an environment that promotes personal growth. Some of the best employees are those who want to continue to grow. Nature is a good analogy to describe the process. As long as something is growing, it stays alive and produces fruit. Once it stops growing, it dies and begins to rot.

People with a "weeder" mindset resist growing and are content to just survive in the workplace. Highly talented and skilled people are attracted to the culture of personal growth, which allows them to excel in their skills and attitude.

Developing leaders is a slow process. When new staff members are hired, they usually get excited about the Leader to Leader classes because most have never experienced anything like it. Over time, that excitement can diminish, and they usually do one of two things.

The wise ones will begin new habits and start working on themselves and quietly set a pace of personal growth. They don't stop growing after the excitement is gone. Their roots, so to speak, start going down deep, which allows them to set a foundation upon which they build something great.

They don't rely on the class to develop themselves; they find ways to grow on their own. They read books, listen to audiobooks, ask to go to conferences, go on site visits, search for resources, network with peers, and even interview other people in order to grow. They become more self-aware, better decision makers, and engaged in making positive changes.

In the second response, while staff members may sense the value of personal growth and get excited about what they're learning in the Leader to Leader classes, they don't embrace it outside the class and don't experience consistent change for long. They return to their old ways of dealing with work and life.

They are often the ones left sitting on the fence, waiting to see which way the wind is blowing to determine their destiny. They wander through life without a plan. Their roots are shallow and susceptible to rough weather. In time, if not careful, they can become jaded and detached. This is a very dangerous state.

Just like a vegetable detached from the plant, they stop growing and will start to rot.

Set Employees Up for Success

"You can have everything in life you want, if you'll just help enough other people get what they want."
—Zig Ziglar, Author and Motivational Speaker

To make the team successful, this may mean working with other departments and contractors. It is important to work with those in charge to make the work of the staff as systematic and low maintenance as possible.

Sometimes making people successful means holding them accountable for their behavior or performance. It is not always easy, but it is part of the growing process. One of the worst ways to lead people is to let a person get away with bad behavior or performance. Others see it and wait for the person in charge to take action. When the leader doesn't do anything, then the staff gets frustrated, and morale and trust drops among the team.

Cross-training staff is a great way to get people to see the bigger picture and be more successful. It helps staff members walk in the shoes of their co-workers and gives them insights into others' jobs. In the landscape department, team members gain a greater appreciation for what it takes to make the campus beautiful. Cross-training helps them gain more knowledge and widen their skills. It also helps stop people from complaining that others' jobs are easier than theirs.

Cross-training also opens the door for others to move up or over in the organization. For instance, we started trying different people at irrigation, and in time, a few key team members surfaced. We now have two full-time irrigation staff.

Mentoring

"I think a role model is a mentor – someone you see on a daily basis, and you learn from them."
—Denzel Washington, Actor

Life is more than cutting grass, pulling weeds, and creating a beautiful outdoor landscape. Life becomes more meaningful when we invest in those around us.

We assign every new person a mentor at work. This sets the tone for learning, listening, and growing. We want all new hires to be successful in what they do. Whether they stay with us or eventually move to a new job, we want them to be successful.

We work hard to foster an environment where full-time staff is empowered to teach our student workers.

Don't Be Intimidated

"Surround yourself with people who are smarter than you."
—Russell Simmons, Chairman & CEO,
Rust Communications

A friend at another university shared a story about interviewing a potential candidate for an entry-level grounds position. The hiring committee learned that the candidate was very qualified and brought many years of landscape experience, having owned his own landscape company. One person on the committee, who also worked in the grounds department, was intimidated by the candidate's knowledge and insights. My friend said the committee didn't hire the qualified candidate, his tone reflecting his disappointment.

While on a hiring committee, I encountered a similar situation. The position was for an entry-level groundskeeper, and one candidate showed strong leadership qualities and plant knowledge. After the interview, one of the committee members asked, "Do we want to hire a leader or a follower? This candidate seems to be more of a leader." Obviously, he did not want the leader.

In both cases, it appeared that a person on the committee was intimidated by someone who knew more and had more experience. It can be a bit unsettling to the status quo to bring in a top talent. Some people get intimidated because of their own insecurities.

When you can admit you don't know everything about your operation but can learn from your staff, you help set the tone that all your staff can learn from one another. **It is very freeing to hire people smarter than you.** It can inspire people to learn, look up solutions to their challenges, and dig deeper into a subject.

Of course, knowledge is not the only factor in hiring, but all things being equal, look for leaders, not weeders.

CHAPTER 7

Growing Leaders, not Weeders

What You Have Is Contagious

"If you love your work, you'll be out there every day trying to do it the best you possibly can, and pretty soon everybody around will catch the passion from you – like a fever."
—Sam Walton, Founder, Wal-Mart

eaders set the tone for the organization. One way they do that is by how they view their own work. **If you love your work and what you do, make sure you tell the people with whom you work.** Better yet, show it. It is contagious. Many people will identify with your passion and see it is OK to be excited about work.

The same holds true for bosses who hate their work. Counting the days tells everyone you would rather be someplace else, and you really do not enjoy what you do. Find what you love to do, that work that drives you to get up every day and want to be there.

Let me pause here and say that you can be employed without passion for your work. You can do all that is expected of you without it, but if you are a leader and you want your staff to be working with you and not for you, then you've got to have passion for what you do.

Passion for your work does not mean jumping around like a "rah-rah" crazy person. It is a desire to be the best, to help others on your team be the best, and share that desire to do something great together.

Monday Morning Meeting

"Take advantage of every opportunity to practice your communication skills so that when important occasions arise, you will have the gift, the style, the sharpness, the clarity, and the emotions to affect other people."
—**Jim Rohn, Author & Motivational Speaker**

Having a department meeting just because you're supposed to have one is a waste of everyone's time. I don't like to have a lot of meetings, but the few that we have, we use them for learning, communications, and leadership development.

In my early days of working at Ole Miss, I would lead the department meetings and did 99 percent of the talking. When I wanted feedback, the meetings became painful as staff had been conditioned not to talk. When I asked someone to give an update or share information, I saw uncomfortable fidgeting and blank stares. My goal was to develop leaders, not weeders, so I had to get my direct reports to participate.

Very few if any of the staff members had ever spoken in front of the entire department in a meeting, and they were very hesitant to speak. As each supervisor was asked to report what was going on in their areas, they would say, "There is nothing to report, all is good." To say this frustrated me would be an understatement.

Supervisors and I met prior to our department meetings with the goal of developing their confidence in speaking in front of everyone. We constantly discussed how important it is to pass along information, to be open, and not to assume everyone knows or remembers information.

It took lots of practice, being persistent, and at times it was like pulling teeth. In time, they got much better at sharing information from their areas, and it soon became the new normal in our department meetings. Their confidence was growing.

A few years later, it was time to shift responsibilities and let Denise Hill, who was in charge of day-to-day operations, lead the meetings. After about a year or so leading the meetings, she began to have the supervisors not only participate but also lead the entire meetings. At this point, we developed a one-page meeting agenda. Each week, the meeting leader followed the agenda and kept things moving along.

The role of running the meeting evolved into some good leadership development. As staff members grew in their leadership skills, we looked for ways to involve everyone in the department meetings. Each person was assigned a week to lead the meetings. At first, we saw a little pushback, but we started with some staff who embraced the idea and did a great job. The staff members got used to their new role, and it has become routine.

Each time a person finishes leading the meeting, we all clap and show appreciation. We have announcements, then supervisors talk about their areas, and we talk about plant identification and safety.

The more people speak, the more they feel ownership and build their leadership skills. I'm amazed how over time we changed the tone of our meetings to be more engaging. My speaking part in the meetings these days is down to 5 percent.

Each person on the team also received a calendar and is expected to bring it to all meetings.

We mark important dates for maintenance, service dates, holidays, ballgames, crew birthdays, finals, and other big events on campus. We also add who will lead the meetings, who will teach plant identification, who has the safety topic, and inspiring quotes. One page even has a place to write down personal goals. As simple as it is, the calendar is a good way to stay in the loop and see the big picture.

Field Trips

"Tell me and I forget. Teach me and I remember. Involve me and I learn."
—Benjamin Franklin

It takes assistance from others to build leaders. When I first came to Ole Miss, Chancellor Khayat said I needed to visit Vanderbilt University in Nashville to see how its campus looked. At that time, he thought Vanderbilt had done some good landscaping work that Ole Miss could emulate. So I visited and spoke with my peers there.

Within a year, five staff supervisors and I went on a weeklong trip to visit Vanderbilt, University of Louisville, University of Kentucky, and several other properties to see and compare the landscapes. These trips were highly valuable to our development.

The next year, several of us traveled to the University of Alabama, Auburn University, Calloway Gardens, The Grove Landscape Co. in Atlanta, and Georgia Tech. In time, we made it down to LSU, Texas A&M, University of Texas, and Southern Methodist University.

In the winter, we scheduled trips to Mississippi universities and community colleges because we could see them in one day.

Every trip, I reminded the staff to be open and see the site like a new parent. I asked what made an impression on them, what they liked and disliked.

These trips have saved us countless dollars by seeing what others are doing right and differently. Our landscape staff has learned about other universities' standards and training for their properties. They have learned what questions to ask when they visit other universities, as well as to listen, observe, and learn from others.

I'll be honest. We don't have time to travel. We are extremely busy, just like most people. But these trips are well worth the time, energy, and investment. I would do them all again without hesitation. I plan to keep doing them.

Our staff members still refer to things they saw, learned, and people they have met. Our team discovered it shares many of the same challenges as its counterparts at other universities. **Coach your team to be leaders by asking, listening, and learning.**

Speakers

"No matter what people tell you, words and ideas can change the world."
—Robin Williams, Comedian

One way to help cultivate greatness in your employees is to invite speakers to talk to them. Being on a college campus, Landscape Services has access to some interesting people. Faculty members come speak to our group for 5 to 10 minutes to tell us about what they do and how our landscaping work affects them. This pays dividends because the crew members hear about the value they bring to campus.

Alumni such as Larry Martindale visit and share how he went from being an impoverished Tennessee farm boy to coming to Ole Miss on a basketball scholarship and later becoming successful in the business world. Such stories inspire our team members and help them to understand their role in making Ole Miss the most beautiful campus they can.

When special guests come speak, it's helpful to prepare your team. It is normal for most of us to be a little shy or hesitant to ask questions or go up and say hello after the event. It's helpful to explain why the speaker is coming and how having him or her speak benefits the team.

It's also useful to review what questions to ask. In our department, we do role playing before the speaker arrives to familiarize everyone with what our time with the guest speaker might be like. This helps show them how to be professional in this setting.

Paid speakers also can be a great tool to initiate conversation and as a springboard for change. They have helped our staff learn insights, work through tough challenges, and confirm our direction.

The first 12 months I was on campus, I was fortunate enough to attend a two-day leader training class with the landscape front-line supervisors. The biggest takeaway was after the training, when we were able to build on the knowledge we learned in a small group meeting. It cost a few dollars and days, but we learned to collaborate better, found our direction, and started developing our core values.

Conferences and Trade Shows

"I never learn anything talking. I only learn things when I ask questions."
—Lou Holtz, American Football Coach, and Analyst

Taking staff to conferences can be a great way to expose them to bigger thinking and what is new in your industry. Prepare your team members before each trip about what to expect, what they need to look for, and how to engage in the event.

Encourage your team to be interviewers when they meet people. Most people are eager to talk about what they do. Tell staff members not to worry about telling people what they do, just ask questions and listen.

Asking staff members to come back from conferences with answers to problems gives them a focus and reason for going. They come back with new contacts with whom they can network. I specifically joined a professional organization to help fast-track our learning and networking opportunities. The Professional Grounds Management Society has been a super investment.

Leaders need to coach their team on the best ways to be successful.

Personal Goals

"Great leaders help their people see how they can directly impact the company's objectives and their own personal goals."
—Chip Conley, Author

Most people never meet their goals in life because they are not clear on what their goals are.

Personal goals can help at work. For instance, an employee who sets a personal goal to lose weight and succeeds is going to feel better, be healthier, gain confidence, and see him or herself as making progress in life. This helps the employee as well as the company.

In Landscape Services, we use the first page of the calendar as a space for individuals to set goals. I don't think everyone sets goals, but many do. About once a quarter, the team members review their goals. If they fail at a goal, they are encouraged to see it as just another starting point. Personal goals help people lead themselves to the next level.

Walk Alongside Your Team

"If you want to make a difference in the lives of the people you lead, you must be willing to walk alongside them, to lift and encourage them, to share moments of understanding with them, and to spend time with them, not just shout down at them from on high."
—Tony Dungy, Former Head Football Coach for the Indianapolis Colts

The first several years I was on campus, I kept hearing employees were surprised I was in the field with them. For most of my career, I have gotten out and engaged with team members, letting them know I appreciate their work. The saying that people respect what you inspect is true.

Special meals are also scheduled a few times a year. Those meals are a great way to build goodwill and connect with staff. Sometimes, I help with preparation or cleanup, and I always go to the back of the line and fill my plate toward the end. I want to set the example that leaders serve. **I am here for their success; they are not here for my success.**

I make sure staff members know my office door is open for the good and the bad. If they have a problem and need to talk about it, they can. This has proven to be useful to help clear the air and open up communications. We call these "venting sessions."

At the end of the day, I sometimes walk through and talk to the crew members about their day. At times, I shake hands or fist bump with each team member. I may look each person in the eye and say a few encouraging words. That one moment, we pause and shake hands as people who respect and appreciate each other for what we stand for and do every day. It's so brief, but **as the leader, if I am not validating the work they do, who is?** For me, it is meaningful to be able to share that bond with the team.

Laugh Olympics

"There is little success where there is little laughter."
—Andrew Carnegie, American
Industrialist

Over the years, our team has participated in fun team-building events. We call one such event Laugh Olympics, which includes egg tosses, pine straw races, and a mowing course. We have done the ropes course on campus too. All this is to continue to cultivate a team atmosphere and enjoy one another in a different light.

Check Out the Library

"Successful people are always looking for opportunities to help others. Unsuccessful people are always asking, 'What's in it for me?'"
—Brian Tracy, Author & Speaker

While doing Leader to Leader classes, where we had many great discussions, we started incorporating videos from Ted Talks and books from authors such as John Maxwell, Les Brown, and Zig Ziglar. A common theme was the value of personal growth, or if you want to see change in your life, start working on you first.

One of our best free resources to help people grow is the local library. When Landscape Services staff members and I first went to the local library, and I was happy to see so many of the team get library cards, and some went ahead and checked out audiobooks while we were there. When team members invest in themselves, they become a better team.

CHAPTER 8

Weeding by Example

"The action that made the most difference was setting a personal example."
—Idan Bar-Sade, Author

Chancellor Khayat had invited me to his home the first week I started work at Ole Miss. He wanted to walk the campus with me early in the morning, way before any students were stirring. As was his ritual, he left early each morning to walk the campus for the exercise, exchange greetings with staff, and check on things. While walking, he would pick up litter and even pull a weed or two.

With his unique leadership style, Khayat took tremendous ownership in the Ole Miss campus. He cared for it, loved it, and did all he could to make it better. He tried to see the campus like a first-time parent. He knew one of Ole Miss' assets was an aesthetically pleasing campus. He wanted to capitalize on that beauty in all areas of the campus.

The chancellor and I started walking out of his driveway, and within minutes he had spotted a piece of litter and stopped to pick it up. It didn't take me long to spot my first piece of litter too, so I copied what I had seen him do. But his actions did not surprise me because I had been told by many people that this was normal for him. He was known for leading by example, even in the smallest of details.

Years later, I realized that his actions had affected me in a deeper way. **He did it because it needed to be done, and he wasn't going to walk past something that needed attention.** In our conversations, he related that having a clean campus reflects our image to the world. He told me that while growing up, his mother had said to him, "Make a place look loved."

Khayat was never afraid to get his hands dirty, which earned him the respect of our staff. I mentioned I had seen him pull a weed or two and said he was "weeding by example."

Because he had such ownership in making Ole Miss successful, I believe it gave him more influence with many he met. Once on campus, I saw him, dressed in a suit and tie, pull his car over and pick up a bag of litter in the middle of street. He practiced what he preached.

Practice What You Preach

"An ounce of practice is worth more than tons of preaching."
—Mahatma Gandhi

People want to know that the person they are following is someone they can trust, a person who lives out what they say. Setting an example is all about carrying it out. No one enjoys working with a hypocrite, a person who says one thing and does something else.

If you want crape myrtle trees to be selectively pruned and all you do is sever them, you are not practicing what you preach. If you believe that your team needs to be organized, then you need to be organized. If you value staff not calling in sick when they just don't feel like going to work, then don't call in sick when you're not sick.

When you practice what you preach, you earn the respect of those with whom you work. They know they can trust you and you're doing the work with them. If you expect the team to be working in the field, but you go to your office to play on the computer and goof off, you destroy your credibility, even when you don't get caught goofing off. It affects you mentally because you know you're not doing your part for the team. People want to know they can trust you to do your part.

You choose how you lead. You can go to work, meet the minimum requirements, and survive in your job. You can bark out orders and run roughshod over people. You can be deceitful and play games with people's emotions, play one crew off another and be divisive. (This is ugly.)

How you lead yourself is a reflection on you, those you work with, and your organization. It even carries over to those you love outside the workplace. In the big picture, the way you lead yourself becomes your reputation. You choose how you lead yourself every minute of every day.

Cultivate Respect

"If you accept others for who they are, they're more likely to accept you for who you are."
**—Sam Haskell, Executive Chairman,
Miss America Organization**

A while ago, I overheard a custodian talking about a certain leadership style. She was describing a leader in such clear and relatable terms, it made me stop and smile. She said, "If (a leader) treats you like he wants to be treated, then people will want to work for him, but if he doesn't give a crap about you, then nobody wants to stay and work for him."

It's a simple matter of treating people with respect and wanting to be treated with respect. We watch how people treat us, talk to us, or ignore us.

I noticed Chancellor Khayat on his early morning walks on campus would speak to people. He had things to do, places to go, but he never hesitated to smile or interact with staff, contractors, visitors, even protestors, as he walked the grounds.

Leaders who make eye contact, smile, use a firm handshake, and are not afraid to engage in conversation are the ones who are going to be more effective at work and, more importantly, change lives.

Leaders can add passion and fuel, or they can drain all the energy away. I have seen leaders who think and act as if they are better than their co-workers. These are the energy drainers. Most people will like their work based on how much they like their boss.

But respect goes even deeper. Cultivating a culture where people respect one another is the foundation of building a winning team. Like in sports, you focus on the goals of the team. The deeper you can build respect, the better the team will be.

The Golden Rule

> *"My favorite parable for living a positive and influential life is the Golden Rule: 'Do unto others what you would have them do unto you.'"*
> **—Tony Oller, singer**

As simple as it sounds, the Golden Rule is often an overlooked key to leading and working with teams. **Listen. Better yet, give people an opportunity to speak.** Over the years, I have found that most folks want to like their work, want to do a good job, and want to get along with fellow workers. I find leading by example means treating people the way I want to be treated.

As described in Capt. D. Michael Abrashoff's audiobook *It's Your Ship, Management Techniques from the Best Damn Ship in the Navy*, people at the top of the leadership chain of command don't always listen to the team. Most top leaders are not told what is happening on the ground level, which means they don't know what's really going on.

Like monkeys sitting in a tree, one monkey is at the top of the tree looking down on all the other monkeys looking up at him. All that monkey sees is the smiling faces looking up at him. Meanwhile, the monkeys looking up have a different perspective. They don't see smiling faces.

In Landscape Services, I try to move down in the tree, look up, look across, listen, and work with the staff. After listening to Abrashoff's book, I started doing one-on-one sessions with the people in our department. It takes time. It slows us down, it can be awkward, feel like a waste of time, but it's still worth it. It helps make our organization flatter and me more approachable. People appreciate that I try to get to know them and listen to them. It costs little to do, but it pays back dividends.

Some of the best ideas come from the front-line staff. At times when we meet, it inspires ideas. Short meetings provide bursts of energy and allow people to participate in finding solutions and making us better. If people don't want to talk about their ideas or suggestions in a group, they can write them down and leave them in the "inspiration" box.

The box gets a few suggestions for changes or improvements several times a year. If we can act on these immediately, then we do. If they involve greater detail or are out of our control, then we explore the best course of action and circle back to the person who made the suggestion. People want to know you're listening.

Simply put, treat people with respect if you want to be respected.

When you lead by example, you are setting your standards high, you are taking the high road. This is especially valuable when you hire new employees. In our department, we try to tap into how people felt their first day on the job with us: a little anxious and unsure of what to expect. Then we encourage our existing staff members to remember those who were friendly to them and to do the same thing for the new person. Be the leader, reach out, and treat them the way you want to be treated.

Honesty, according to *The Leadership Challenge* by Kouzes & Posner, is the most admired trait in a leader. It allows people to put their trust in you and know you do what is right. The same goes for employees. **When team members say they did their work and you know they are honest, it saves you time because you know it's completed.** If they say the job is done and you're really not sure if they embrace your standards, then you have to verify their work is done right, which decreases productivity.

Attitude

"Change your thoughts and you change your world."
—Norman Vincent Peale, American
Minister & Author

The attitude of a leader is very similar to that of a rock dropped in a pond. His or her attitude ripples through the organization, good or bad. If I get a little moody or have meltdowns, then I affect my team.

I have seen leaders justify these poor outbursts and think everyone understands them. They may think it is OK because they are the boss, and maybe no one has the courage or freedom to let them know, but their moodiness and/or bad attitude is rippling through the organization and negatively affecting its operation. The leader's attitude sets the atmosphere of the team.

My former workout trainer once tapped me on the shoulder and pointed to a man working out in front of the dumbbell rack. It is common courtesy when working out to move away from the dumbbell rack to let others access the weights. This one guy was crowding the rack and blocking others. My trainer said as he pointed to him, "Don't be that guy." Meaning, don't be one of those employees who are so focused on themselves that everyone else has to wait on them, tolerate them and work around them.

Sign Your Work

> *"I love getting to do what I do."*
> **—Denise Hill, University of Mississippi**
> **Superintendent/Landscape Services**

One of our staff, Nathan Lazinsky, expressed a unique way of thinking about what we do each day at work.

"When we do our work, it's like we are signing our name to an important document," he said.

I like that. It is a reflection of who we are. Just as artists are known by their masterpieces, we are known by our beautiful living masterpieces on campus. **The way in which people do their work tells a lot about them. It is their signature to the world.** If we do our work with excellence, it reflects great pride in what we do, and our signature has greater value.

CHAPTER 9

Celebrating the Harvests

Clarify the Win

"Even the best team can't score if it can't find home plate."
—Andy Stanley, Pastor & Leadership
Speaker

W e all like to have wins in our lives. We like our favorite teams to win, our kids to win, and we like personal wins. If our kids get an A on a test or if they learn right from wrong, it is a win. But how do we determine wins in the workplace?

For business owners, winning may have some form of financial gain tied to it. In the nonprofit world, successful fundraising is a win. But what other factors does an organization look at to determine a win?

For some, having a job is their win, but what about those who go beyond just having a job, those who are driven to excellence, those who want to make a difference in the world? What are their wins? Is it being busy all day, answering emails, shuffling papers, and accomplishing the next to-do item?

Who determines the win? If you're the boss, chances are your team is watching to see what tasks and actions get rewarded to determine what a win is. Your team may be defining the win differently from how you define it.

When good leaders get out front and clarify the win for the organization, then the organization is positioned toward focused results or getting the right wins. To put it simply, a win is our scorecard, a way for us to know if we are winning. The clearer our wins are defined, the better we are at getting them. It is much easier to hit a target you can see.

I first heard the term "clarify the win" from Leadercast speaker and pastor Andy Stanley. He said, "Even the best team can't score if it can't find home plate." What I found insightful was the way Stanley stressed the importance of clearly defining wins at every level of the organization. This has helped our department find home plate in a confusing and busy ballpark.

It is easy to look on the scoreboard at any point in a football game and determine who is winning. But how does a landscape services organization determine if it is winning or losing? If it is only financial, we've stayed on budget; however, we may win the numbers game but lose the campus appearance game.

Our customers are not determining our wins by our budget. They determine our wins by how the campus looks, how they relate to it while they are there.

In the landscape world of never-ending growth cycles and projects, our days are busy with many tasks and to-do lists. Add such challenges as weather, the needs of the campus, upgrades, new construction, mishaps, staffing, training, and scheduling, and there is a lot to balance.

This is true in any industry, which is why we need to clarify what a win is. It is easy to stay busy every moment of the day, do each task, and check it off the list. Defining the wins lets us become laser focused on what is important.

Our wins are defined through people, processes, product, and purpose, e.g., staff staying on schedule with our campus maintenance calendar or mentoring student workers; having people share how much they appreciate the landscaping on campus or that they came to Ole Miss because of the beauty of the campus. All of these wins add up to creating the most beautiful campus, the big win.

If you are the leader of your organization, then you have an important role to play in clarifying the win. Left undefined, others will do what they believe is a win. Though they may do something good, it may take the organization off course and expend unnecessary energy and resources.

The organizational leader accepts his/her role as defining wins with and for the team by initiating the conversation and seeing it through. It surely doesn't mean he or she does it alone, but the leader needs to take on the responsibility to start defining the wins.

When Coach Hugh Freeze became the head football coach at Ole Miss, he brought a very simple phrase with him, **"Win the Day."** I really like this because winning the day takes the focus to win every day and not just winning one big game on Saturday.

For my department, is going outside and working on the landscape a win for us? No. Is mowing the lawn areas a win? No. Those tasks are important but are not laser focused to create a bigger win.

For us to win at mowing, we examine our process and create an efficient model we want followed each day. By following this model, staff stays on schedule at a high level, thus getting the win. The process and schedule are ways to ensure we do the key task needed to make the campus beautiful and help people to connect with the university.

As our staff members participate in Landscape University, they learn the knowledge, skills, and attitude to complete the processes. This gives our people the win. The win is not being busy or rushing daily to handle urgent tasks; it is to have a plan and be able to implement the plan according to our standards.

Celebrate Big Wins

"Celebrate what you want to see more of."
—Tom Peters, Co-Author "In Search of Excellence"

In 2013, we held a surprise VIP event for our landscape staff to celebrate and say thank you for the four national awards the department had received over the years. Only a few key team members were in on what was going on. To ensure all the staff were present that day and without spoiling the surprise, we started building up the VIP event during our Monday morning meetings.

"You do not want to miss this special day coming up," we would say. "If you miss a day, don't miss this one. It's going to be unique." These announcements added some anticipation, especially as the date got closer. The staff members had fun guessing and hoping we would slip up and tell them the surprise, but we didn't slip up, and everyone showed up.

On the day of the event, beautiful tablecloths, silverware, ceramic plates, and nice centerpieces were arranged at each table, and the meal was catered. Excitement was in the air, but the weather did not cooperate. Heavy rain and wind made having the event in our open-air truck shed at our landscape facility a real challenge. We had a roof over our heads, but no walls.

We talked about having the meal in our break room, but it was too small to accommodate all the staff and guests we invited, and it was going to mess up the surprise I had for the end.

So our landscape team began to figure out ways to adapt and overcome the challenge. In a few minutes, the team came up with a creative solution to stop the rain from blowing in. We had access to large pieces of equipment, and someone suggested that two large box trucks, the large chipper truck, and two large garbage trucks could be used to create a makeshift wall on both sides of the shed to block the rain. It worked, and I was very relieved and proud of the staff's creative thinking and teamwork.

During the celebration, former Chancellor Dan Jones, Vice Chancellor Larry Sparks, and Athletics Director Ross Bjork each spoke and congratulated the team on its success.

Our university event coordinator, Christine Wallace, made arrangements to give a special pewter and glass paperweight, with the four national awards inscribed on it, to each staff member. Each employee was announced as he or she walked up to the front to receive a trophy, and was greeted by the guests and given a big hug from landscape administrator Bonnie Black.

After all the staff had eaten, heard the speeches, received their trophies, and were lingering around the front stage where we had just taken our team photo, it was time to unveil the last surprise. I picked up the microphone and began to recap each of the national award years. While reading, I nodded to two of our mechanics to pull a cord from the top of the truck shed. Each cord released a national championship banner.

Just like championship banners hung in a football stadium or basketball arena, four banners hung from the rafters to be permanent reminders to our staff members of their accomplishments thus far. Days after the event, crew members boasted about being a part of something unique and nationally recognized.

Celebrate Personal Wins

"A soldier will fight long and hard for a bit of colored ribbon."
—**Napoleon Bonaparte**

National championships are big wins, but we also celebrate individual wins. We celebrate those who continue to train and become certified. The Landscape University certification program provides a way for front-line staff to earn internal certification. We also celebrate certifications earned from other organizations such as the International Society of Arborists. We recognize those accomplishments with a small reception, where we present a certificate, a magnet for the employee's locker, and usually apparel such as a cap or shirt.

The Product

"Most businesses think that product is the most important thing, but without great leadership, mission and a team that deliver results at a high level, even the best product won't make a company successful."
—**Robert Kiyosaki, Business Leader**

We are truly grateful when people identify with the product we produce – the beauty of the campus landscaping – and reach out to say how much they admire and appreciate it. When we get an email or letter from someone complimenting the hard work, we read it in our meetings, post it on the board, and talk about what an honor it is to receive these kind words. It is a win when a team member gets kudos because someone read his/her shirt or jacket that says Ole Miss Landscape Services.

We encourage our team to share these compliments. It is a great way to remind our team members how the community views their hard work. These golden moments reinforce the message that they are important and what they do matters.

CHAPTER 10

Growing the Legacy of Leadership

"The greatest legacy one can pass on to one's children and grandchildren is not money or other material things accumulated in one's life, but rather a legacy of character and faith."

—Billy Graham, America Evangelist

believe we all have God-given talents. How we use those talents will be our legacy. I'm confident that Michael Jordan's legacy is secure as being one of the greatest basketball players of all time. U.S. presidents have created legacies from their time in office. Managers and leaders at every level will leave legacies, good or bad.

In one of our Leader to Leader classes, a team member said it well, "We have a birth date and a death date and a dash in between the two dates." **How well you live your dash is what is important.**

Having these conversations with our team from time to time helps bring perspective and big-picture thinking to our lives and work. It allows us to pause for a minute and reflect on "What do I want to be known for?"

I have been encouraged over the years as I hear team members take this to heart, watch the way they treat people, and see their work change for the good as this message sinks in. To work at a place for 10, 20, 30 years and see the same people each day, people get to know you. What will these people remember about you when you are gone?

Time Is Limited

"If you think in terms of a year, plant a seed; if in terms of ten years, plant trees; if in terms of 100 years, teach the people."
—Confucius

In our Leader to Leader classes, we have had some great discussions on how important our role is on campus. Staff members connect the dots from what they do to how it affects other departments and our university.

These discussions lead to clarity when it comes to determining priorities and how we do things. When we are doing our work and are asked to turn off our equipment because students are taking exams, we do it. We even try not to be around buildings with loud equipment where exams are taking place. The takeaway lesson is to serve others in ways that help them be successful.

It is vital that all our staff members know their role is important to the success of Ole Miss, but at some point along the way, we will all be replaced. The campus started in 1848, and a lot of employees have come and gone in that time.

This takes us to some great conversations of legacy and what do you want to be known for at work and even at home.

Having these open discussions makes us face our mortality and know it is not all about "me." We are a small part of something unique and big. We get to see young people come on campus to develop and aspire to do more with their lives.

In a small way, we are a part of each student's life, having created and maintained that unique outdoor environment. We help create the environment that attracts, retains, and produces graduates, some of whom are destined for greatness, who will lead others well.

To feel like they are saving their job, some people are reluctant to teach others how to do it. They believe they will no longer be needed and will be replaced. But good people who can train are always needed. **The person who has a closed mind about helping others is the one who will be replaced.**

When I first came to Ole Miss, one employee constantly told me how he was the only person who could do many of the tasks in the department. In his mind, he was the indispensable man. Former French President Charles de Gaulle said, "Our graveyards are full of indispensable men."

Create a Creed

"A people without the knowledge of their past history, origin and culture is like a tree without roots."
—Marcus Garvey, American Journalist

Years ago, motivational speaker and retired Green Beret Terry Johnson came to speak to our team. Johnson did a wonderful job of teaching and inspiring our group. As part of the session, he quoted the Green Beret Creed by heart.

We shared with Johnson all we were doing with our creation of Landscape University, the classes, the special training, and attention to details. He said he was inspired by our work and encouraged us to create our own creed for our department. When I heard him say it, I really did not give it a lot of thought, but his words never left my mind.

Our department was really beginning to gain momentum in many areas, and lots of good things were happening. I began to see success in areas of leadership and staff members who were growing in their personal journeys. I remembered Johnson's suggestion about creating a creed, and it seemed like the right time to try it. I began mentioning it to key leaders in our department and in our Leader to Leader classes to get a feel for the idea. No one seemed super excited, but no one really opposed it either.

One wintry day, we scheduled a 60-minute meeting of the entire staff to walk through the process of developing our very own Landscape Creed. The key was to let everyone participate in some way in helping to create the Landscape Creed. We passed around examples of a few creeds and showed a few videos of teams reciting their creeds.

The most stirring videos we watched came from the U.S. military. The conviction to serve, adapt, and overcome had some values to which we could relate. We are not the military, but in a few areas, we feel we share some of the same core values.

Our team was asked: What do you want to be known for? What do you want the new staff members to understand about our department? It was like turning on a fire hydrant. The statements flowed, and we filled up several big sheets of notes.

It was a great start, but it was time to go back out in the field and get our work done. While everyone had a voice at the first meeting, the next meeting was set up as voluntary.

Well over half the crew came to the second meeting. The synergy was incredible, and I was fired up, hearing all the great input from our team. Staff members were working on this when they went home and brought rough drafts to share with the team.

We refined the creed a little more each time we met over the next several weeks. Each time, we found phrases and words we liked and didn't like. Each time, our values got a little clearer. I knew we were working on something bigger than ourselves, but little did I realize the influence this creed would have on our future.

Landscape Creed

We, the Department of Landscape Services, are a team of hardworking individuals united under one banner and dedicated to inspiring others.

We …

Lead by Example.
Adapt and Overcome.
Never Stop Training and Growing.
Dedicate Ourselves to Professional Integrity.
Serve with Respect and Pride.
Cultivate Greatness.
Achieve Quality Results with an Eye for Detail.
Promote and Provide a Beautiful Environment.
Excel through High Standards and Excellence Within.

I am a Landscape Rebel.

Every week, we say the Ole Miss Landscape Creed to conclude our Monday morning meeting. The purpose of saying it is to remind us of our core values. We share the creed the first day with new staff and student workers to introduce them to our department culture. Many of our staff have committed it to memory.

When we live these words out, great things happen in the landscape.

We lead by example is the foundation for leadership, and the first person we lead is ourselves. The way we do this determines much about us personally and professionally. This is empowering and eye-opening to many people who never see themselves as a leader.

Adapt and overcome gives us the mindset of how we do things. We may start mowing today, and a thunderstorm comes up. Do we simply stop working and stand around until the storm is over? We adapt and overcome by going to plan B. We know bad weather is always a possibility, so the plan is to have many items we can do when it happens. Most of the time, the crew simply puts on the rain gear and moves ahead. If that doesn't work, there is always training, cleaning, servicing, organizing, developing classes, and going on field trips.

Letting our team slip into the mindset of defeat is devastating to morale and lowers our standards. Even when we get hit with an unexpected item (a zinger as we call it), we have a mindset to adapt and work through it. We know zingers are a part of our culture – expect the unexpected. In Landscape University, we created a class that teaches how we overcome and handle zingers. The mindset of adapting and overcoming has to be planted, cultivated, and grown to become second nature.

Never stop training and growing is one of my favorite lines because it reminds us that when a tree is alive and producing fruit, it is growing. When it dies, it stops growing and rots.

As individuals, we need to be undergoing some type of personal growth to challenge ourselves to be better for our families and for work. That was a big reason our staff members have visited the local library and been exposed to great teachers, to help foster their interest in their personal growth. Several of our team have truly embraced listening to audiotapes and reading books. I have seen real change in their lives, how they carry themselves, taking responsibility for their actions.

Dedicating ourselves to professional integrity sets the tone for doing our work at a high standard and not taking shortcuts. We are professionals. We are committed to learning and doing our jobs the right way. It is easy to skip over items, take little shortcuts, but in the end, they usually come back to slow us down and can cost us more time, energy, and money. In Landscape University, we teach our standards so staff doesn't just rely on what the supervisor or someone else decides that day. After we started teaching our standards in Landscape U, I was amazed to see the staff's confidence grow.

No longer was the pressure on me or any of the other leaders to enforce the standards. Staff members know what is expected and hold each other accountable.

We serve with respect and pride reminds us that to serve is an honor and great privilege. The university needs our services every day, and we are fortunate to do it. Former Ole Miss Chancellor Dan Jones reminded the campus years ago that the University of Mississippi leads and excels by engaging minds, transforming lives, and *serving* others. Every job is honorable and noble. Don't let anyone put you down because of what you do. Be the best at what you do, whatever it is. Martin Luther King Jr. said it well:

> *"If a man is called to be a street sweeper, he should sweep streets even as Michelangelo painted, or Beethoven composed music or Shakespeare wrote poetry. He should*

sweep streets so well that all the hosts of heaven and earth will pause to say, 'Here lived a great street sweeper who did his job well.'"

Cultivating Greatness is our vision. We added it to our creed to remind us of the big picture of what we do every day. We encourage greatness both outside in the landscaping and inside each person.

Achieve quality results with an eye for detail defines what we want and how. We want to be thorough about the little things to produce high-caliber work. An eye for detail is a way to say pay attention and excel to our level of quality. There is a right way. Look to see if it meets our standards. See the challenges, don't ignore them. Landscape University classes helped get new staff and students up to speed and holding them accountable in having quality work.

Promote and provide a beautiful environment. Ultimately, this is why our department exists. Promoting is being proactive, not waiting to be told what to do every second of the day. Have enthusiasm for your work. It is the mindset of a winner. When we take care of the details, providing a beautiful environment takes care of itself.

Excel through high standards and excellence within reminds us that we have standards, and we do our work with mastery. High standards need to be clear and defined in each area of work. It's important to know what standards you are following.

Before we had Landscape University, we had crews doing work but with inconsistent standards. This affected quality and uniformity of the end product. Once we started getting the crews involved in creating the standards we wanted to achieve, the standards became uniform and our consistency was incredibly higher. Because they have the desire to be the best, the crew members rarely lowered the standards; instead, they raised them.

I am a Landscape Rebel. This connects our department to Ole Miss and reminds us that we are part of a larger team, striving for excellence.

I hope this book has in some way inspired and given you some ideas to add value to you and your team. Never underestimate the value you bring to your organization and vital role you play. Most people fear getting out of their comfort zone, but not you. You will be one of the few who cultivates greatness in yourself and those around you. I look forward to one day meeting you and hearing of your success.

In the following pages you can read about the successes of some of our *Weeding Leaders*. I hope these stories inspire you as they have me.

ABOUT THE AUTHOR

Doing more with less is a 21st century mandate and no one knows this better than a Director of Landscape Services. Jeff McManus, CGM, has found unique ways of meeting that mandate by developing a dedicated, thoughtful and inspiring work force. Jeff's GROW-Theory, which is based in the belief that all humans either strive for or have within them the elements of Greatness, Resiliency, Opportunity and Wisdom, has been fruitful on the Ole Miss campus. McManus and his team created the Landscape University™ for intrinsically motivating employees personally, while training them professionally.

Jeff has a bachelor's degree in Landscape and Ornamental Horticulture from Auburn University and is the recipient of the 2016 Horticulture Alumni of the year. He is also an International

Society of Arboriculture Certified Arborist. Jeff has been with the University of Mississippi since 2000 as Director of Landscape Services. During those years Jeff and his team have gained national recognition for their attention to detail and eye for beauty. Under Jeff's leadership the Ole Miss campus has won the National Professional Grounds Maintenance Society Best Maintained Campus twice, Newsweek's most beautiful campus in 2011 and was named by the Princeton Review as the 2013 most beautiful campus. Jeff led his team in some creative waste management, which caught the attention of The New York Times, November 1, 2014.

Jeff, a native of Georgia, lives in Oxford, Mississippi with his wife and four sons. He is a popular speaker and trainer for local, state and national organizations and industry. His first book *Pruning Like A Pro* has garnered attention for its fun and simple approach to the gardener's dilemma…pruning! *Growing Weeders into Leaders* is a labor of love, focusing on the people rather than the plants.

www.jeffmcmanusspeaking.com

OUR WEEDING LEADERS

Denise Hill

You may remember Denise from Chapter 2. She is still a shining example of our GROW theory – that every person has within them the potential for Greatness, Resiliency, Opportunity and Wisdom. They just need the right conditions to access the potential within.

Denise had worked for Landscape Services only a few months before I noticed her expertise at the helm of her line trimmer. Her polite demeanor and exceptional customer service was second only to the pride she took in her work. She stood out among the staff because she had the eye for detail, the ability to fulfill a vision as well as energize and engage her teammates.

During the following months I challenged Denise with opportunities to lead others – first through training a crew and finally through leading as superintendent of Landscape Services. As one of a very few female crewmembers operating on the grounds, the challenges were large. At each step she found the courage and the skill to gently lead a mostly male crew…then a mostly male department…and now, she serves as my voice on the grounds as superintendant.

As this book prepares to go to print, Denise prepares to return back to work after a winning battle with cancer. As always, she met the challenge with grace, skill and courage and we warmly welcome her back to the team.

Lloyd "Mac" McManus

I tried several times to convince Mac that this was very hands on front line work; the kind with long days that make you sweat and get sun burned. He didn't shy away. He said, I am fine with that, I'm not afraid of getting dirty and I grew up on hard work. Mac joined our landscape team as an entry level employee, with a four-year college degree. He embraced our values of working smarter and not harder by helping us create friendly mowing patterns that allowed our mowers and crews to be more efficient. Mac added great value with his people skills and empowering his crew.

As our department got more efficient we were being asked to do more. The UM Administration needed us to take over the Airport Fixed Base operations at our University airport. The contractor running the FBO had lost the confidence of many customers. We needed someone with efficient leadership.

Running the University Airport was a big job, an additional 200 acres to maintain, fueling planes, embracing customer service skills, plus the responsibility of collecting payment. There were a lot of things that needed leadership. I knew with all we had going on the main campus, that I needed someone I could trust and who could serve this operation with respect and pride. Even though Mac had no previous experience in airport operations, he showed he was willing to learn and take on this large and new adventure. I challenged him that in a few years he should be one of the most knowledgeable persons in the state about airport operations. I encouraged him to be the local expert. Mac didn't shy away. He accepted the tall order.

Today, Mac and his airport team run the second busiest airport in the state and Mac is serving on the Board of the Mississippi Airports Association. Mac hasn't forgotten his roots; recently I caught up with him, jumping off his mower after finishing a few of his 200-acre complex.

David Jumper

He sat in a chair and rattled off a few big name resorts and country clubs he had worked in across the south. He knew his properties, he knew his turf and his resume was impressive. His passion for growing turf grass was in his voice. Was he the one who could take us to the next level and actually help us reduce our mowing schedule? It didn't take long for David Jumper to make his mark on our campus.

Within a few months he had been so proactive in solving our turf issues it could be counted in the number of reduced days mowing. He not only did what I asked, he reached beyond and took initiative to find ways to save us even more time mowing.

David applied a growth regulator on our turf that actually helped slow down the turf growing process and allowed us to keep the campus maintained at a high level. Soon, the Administration asked us to take over the Golf Course Maintenance and day-today pro shop operations. David was a natural fit and jumped at the chance to lead the charge to revamp the course's image.

Today the Ole Miss Golf Course is one of the finest public courses in the region, being voted repeatedly by local golfers as the best course in the area. David models daily his core belief of leading by example as he takes the course to new heights all while operating in the black.

Gerald Barron

As a retired corporate executive, Gerald Barron was a total surprise the day he interviewed to be a groundskeeper. Each person on the committee knew he was over qualified and more than once told him so. Gerald had just moved back to his alma mater, Ole Miss, with his beautiful wife Silva to enjoy retirement in Oxford. Gerald never hesitated in working the long hot days on the Landscape crew. He ran a line trimmer, pulled weeds, trimmed shrubs all for the love of Ole Miss.

After Mac McManus had left to run the Airport, Gerald filled the vacancy as the next supervisor on the north side of campus. Gerald's gentle and understanding approach brought a calm and solidified leadership to our team. He was dedicated to professional integrity by serving his crew and setting them up for success. His wisdom proved vital several times as he helped other leaders with struggles along the way.

Within a few months Gerald was promoted to the Golf Pro Shop Manager and was in charge of all the financial duties. He never changed as a leader with a title. He picked up trash in the parking lot, picked up range balls when needed and never hesitated to get his hands dirty. Our course benefited from his high standards and excellence from within.

Nathan Lazinsky

Nathan Lazinsky was hired as an outside contractor to help with trimming shrubs and trees on our main campus. A former business owner and landscaper, his knowledge and willingness to help grow others led to a full–time hire as a groundskeeper. Nathan quickly brought stability and needed leadership to our detail crew, which oversees our flowers, shrubs and almost anything non turf grass related. He took initiative in the field, creating the Ole Miss magic with our plants. He never stood around waiting to be told what to do and he was highly energized by what he did each day.

As naturally as plants grow and bloom, Nathan learned, grew and blossomed in our culture and adapted to a university property extremely well. After his proven leadership he was given team leadership over all the seasonal color beds and then all the shrubs, small trees and ground cover. His direction as a supervisor grew our teams' plant knowledge. Before long, our people were more capable of figuring out what was right and wrong with a plant. As he continued to grow in his skills he has ably stepped into his role as assistant superintendent in Landscape Services. A role he continues to thrive in today.

A free eBook edition is available with the purchase of this book.

To claim your free eBook edition:
1. Download the Shelfie app.
2. Write your name in upper case in the box.
3. Use the Shelfie app to submit a photo.
4. Download your eBook to any device.

Shelfie

A *free* eBook edition is available
with the purchase of this print book.

CLEARLY PRINT YOUR NAME ABOVE IN UPPER CASE

Instructions to claim your free eBook edition:
1. Download the Shelfie app for Android or iOS
2. Write your name in **UPPER CASE** above
3. Use the Shelfie app to submit a photo
4. Download your eBook to any device

Print & Digital Together Forever.

Snap a photo

Free eBook

Read anywhere

Morgan James makes all of our titles available
through the Library for All Charity Organization.

www.LibraryForAll.org

CPSIA information can be obtained
at www.ICGtesting.com
Printed in the USA
LVOW12s1827031117
554672LV00002BA/2/P